the hand and shov
launching your bu

"People love to dream, imagine, and hope. But even great ideas without action and execution never get off the ground—they don't change the world or your bank account. This book will help identify your ONE sentence, your 'unfair advantage,' and a plan of action to make your idea fly. Spectator or pilot—you get to choose."

"Pat has done the perfect job of inspiring, teaching, motivating and guiding new entrepreneurs through the most important part of the business building process...the fundamentals. However, he goes further, taking us on a journey of discovery, confidence building and support—all with a healthy slice of reality! If you want to get started in online business the smart way, you need to read this book."

"Pat is one of my most trusted resources for Internet business education. Everything he teaches is tested and proven. *Will It Fly?* is no exception. If you want to start an online business then look no further. This book will take you step-by-step through the vetting process so that you can put the odds of success on your side. No smart entrepreneur should consider starting an online business without first running it through *Will it Fly?*"

—**TODD TRESIDDER,** FOUNDER & MONEY COACH AT <u>FINANCIALMENTOR.COM</u>

"It's tempting to create random products and services then HOPE your customers will buy it. However, hope is NOT a strategy. In *Will it Fly?*, Governor Pat Flynn gives you a process to run your ideas through to gain the proof you need to confidently take your idea to market or shelf it before it costs you years, tears, and dollar bills. This is Paperback Business School."

—**JOSH SHIPP,** *INC. MAGAZINE* 30 UNDER 30 ENTREPRENEUR

"I don't know if *Will it Fly?* is the only book of its kind, but I know that I've never read a book like it. Whether you are an entrepreneur who wants to ensure that your next launch is the most successful of your career, or you're a wantrepreneur with an idea that you want to turn into a highly profitable business, this book will give you exactly what you're after."

—**HAL ELROD,** #1 BESTSELLING AUTHOR OF *THE MIRACLE MORNING*

"Our time is the most important resource we have. *Will It Fly?* will help you to turn years of trial and error into mere days by helping you zero in on the business and life decisions that will create the life you want faster. You can bump your head again and again to figure it out, or you can take this incredible guidance from Pat Flynn and start creating the life you desire right now. It really is that powerful."

—**SHAWN STEVENSON,** BESTSELLING AUTHOR AND HOST OF THE MODEL HEALTH SHOW, ITUNES #1 FITNESS & NUTRITION PODCAST

PRAISE FOR *WILL IT FLY?*

"Being an entrepreneur is scary. Especially in the beginning when you feel lonely, lost, and wondering: What if my idea fails? In *Will it Fly?*, Pat Flynn shows you step-by-step how to figure out if your new idea will be successful *before* you go all in. This book is an absolute must-read for any entrepreneur looking to start a new business, enter a new market, or launch a new product. One hundred percent, I recommend reading, and re-reading this book."

—RYAN LEVESQUE, #1 NATIONAL BESTSELLING AUTHOR, *ASK*

"*Will It Fly?* eliminates the number one fear of every new entrepreneur: Will my business idea work? Now you have Pat Flynn acting as your trusted, experienced copilot to help you answer that question. *Will It Fly?* is authentic, as real as it gets, fun to read, and should be required reading for all budding entrepreneurs. Possibly the most important book in your business library."

—RAY EDWARDS, FOUNDER & CEO, RAY EDWARDS INTERNATIONAL, INC.

"Losing your job can be the best thing that ever happens to you. In a short period of time, former employee-turned-entrepreneur Pat Flynn has unlocked the keys to recurring, sustainable income. His new book is inspiring, but that isn't the point—instead of just cheering you on, it will take you by

"I wish I would have read this before launching my writing business. It would have saved me from so many mistakes. If you have an idea you want to share with the world, this book is required reading. Don't miss it."

—JEFF GOINS, BESTSELLING AUTHOR OF *THE ART OF WORK*

" As entrepreneurs, all we have is TIME. Spending our limited bandwidth on a project with its only validation in our own head is a recipe for disaster. In *Will it Fly?*, Pat shares the recipe for SUCCESS. Grow your audience the RIGHT way, by asking for their struggles, constructing the solution in the form of a product/service/community, and create ONLY when they've voted for with their wallet. Pat gives you the ingredients; it's time to take ACTION!"

—JOHN LEE DUMAS, FOUNDER AND HOST OF EOFIRE.COM

"Launching a new product or service can be daunting. Thankfully, Pat Flynn is a knowledgeable guide who will encourage you, show you the essential steps, and help ensure you're on the right path. I wouldn't launch a product without reading this book first."

—DORIE CLARK, AUTHOR OF *STAND OUT* AND *REINVENTING YOU*, AND ADJUNCT PROFESSOR, DUKE UNIVERSITY'S FUQUA SCHOOL OF BUSINESS

HOW to TEST YOUR
NEXT BUSINESS IDEA
so YOU DON'T WASTE
YOUR TIME and MONEY

PAT FLYNN

WILL IT FLY?

HOW *to* TEST YOUR NEXT BUSINESS IDEA *So*

YOU DON'T WASTE YOUR TIME *and* MONEY

-------- *By* --------

PAT FLYNN

FOUNDER *of* <u>SMARTPASSIVEINCOME.COM</u>

IMPORTANT DISCLAIMER

This publication contains materials designed to assist readers in evaluating the merits of business ideas for education purposes only. While the publisher and author have made every attempt to verify that the information provided in this book is correct and up to date, the publisher and author assume no responsibility for any error, inaccuracy, or omission.

ORDERING INFORMATION

Quantity sales. Special discounts are available on quantity purchases by corporations, associations, and others. For details, contact the publisher at the address above.

ISBN 978-0-9970823-0-2: PAPERBACK
ISBN 978-0-9970823-1-9: EBOOK

**WILL IT FLY? HOW TO TEST YOUR NEXT BUSINESS IDEA
SO YOU DON'T WASTE YOUR TIME AND MONEY**

PAT FLYNN

*1. Entrepreneurship. 2. Small Business. 3. Motivational & Inspirational.
4. Validation. 5. How to Start a Business*

EDITING BY COMMAND+Z
BOOK COVER DESIGN BY WINNING EDITS
INTERIOR BOOK DESIGN BY ERIN TYLER
EBOOK DESIGN BY IAN CLAUDIUS

WILL IT FLY?

HOW *TO* TEST YOUR NEXT BUSINESS IDEA *SO* YOU DON'T WASTE YOUR TIME *AND* MONEY

-------- BY --------

PAT FLYNN

SPI PUBLICATIONS, SAN DIEGO

THE FREE

WILL IT FLY? COMPANION COURSE

---------- **WILLITFLYBOOK.COM/STEP1** ----------

To help guide you through *Will It Fly?*, I created a free *Companion Course* that you can get access to which includes downloadable worksheets, bonus video content, and lists of resources and links mentioned in this book. This is your first step toward success with the content in this book, so I highly recommend you sign up now. Inside, the supplemental materials in this free course are organized by the sections and chapters of this book, making it easy for you to find what you need as you read along.

There's also an additional bonus section with content beyond what is shared here in the book, including more case studies and interviews to help you on your journey. I'll be adding more material in this bonus section over time, so make sure to visit the web address below and get free instant access to it now! See you on the inside!

Visit the following link to get free access to your *Will It Fly?* bonus materials now:

---------- **WILLITFLYBOOK.COM/STEP1** ----------

TO

MY **PARENTS**, *for* GIVING ME WINGS...
TO MY **WIFE**, *for* GIVING ME AIR...
TO MY **KIDS**, *for* GIVING ME PURPOSE...

AND TO **YOU**, *for* GIVING IT A CHANCE.

CONTENTS

FOREWORD
(PRE-FLIGHT CHECK)

Besides being one of the most commonly misspelled words in our language, forewords also hold the lofty distinction as one of the most commonly skipped sections in literature.

So why did you land on this page?

Either you are a laudably methodical reader or you still have unanswered questions—*Will this book be worth my time? Why should I care? And can* Will It Fly? *actually help me launch my business idea?*

Let's tackle those one at a time and I promise not to overdo the aviation metaphors while we're still on the runway.

Will this book be worth your time?

First, we all get exactly 168 hours each week. After work and sleep, we're left with about 72 hours that are ours to invest. Have small kids? Then you probably have about half that—weekends and those precious hours after you tuck them in and before you pass out. This is serious calculus. I'm an avid reader, knocking out almost a book a week, and I'm pretty discriminating about the books that make it to my bedside table. I bet you are, too.

Most people read about 200 words a minute and, at that pace, *Will It Fly?* will occupy about $3^1/_2$ hours of your week. That's just a few minutes more than your average NFL game and a lot shorter than your average Netflix binge.

So forgo *House of Cards* for tonight. DVR the game. As I'll explain in answering questions two and three, this book will have a far greater impact on your financial future (and probably result in less snacking, too).

Why should you care?

Like many of you, I primarily know Pat from listening to his podcast. I was introduced to Smart Passive Income about the time we got our dog, Taco. I'm new to this dog business and no amount of research prepared me for all the walking I'd be doing. Mornings and evening, I'd don my ear buds, cue up an episode of Smart Passive Income and hit the streets eager for the next lesson. And often, I'd take the long way so I could enjoy the whole podcast.

I've been in the content business for almost twenty years, first as an editor in New York and now as an author in Austin, and Pat stands out. Pat's action-oriented approach to teaching, his transparency about his successes and failures, and his earnest desire to help others has rightfully won him a huge loyal following (among whom I'm now one). He has not only built successful businesses himself, but has also helped countless others take flight, many of which are documented on the show.

I started reading *Will It Fly?* confident that Pat had some great lessons to impart and that he genuinely wants to help entrepreneurs at the most critical juncture just before takeoff.

Counterintuitively in business and in life, less leads to more. Pat gets this. And there are few more qualified to provide a concise, manageable pre-flight check before your journey.

Can Will It Fly? *actually help you launch your business idea?*

Yes. Pat starts not by scrutinizing your idea, but rather with an exploration of whether the idea is right for you and visa versa. This is a step new entrepreneurs almost universally miss. If you and the idea aren't a true match, you probably won't consider it a success even if it proves financially viable.

A common myth of startup is that it is all about an idea matched with execution. IDEA + EXECUTION = SUCCESS.

The reality is that the missing factor is you (and your partners). YOU + IDEA + EXECUTION = SUCCESS.

After this initial gut check, Pat will walk you through a series of steps to test your idea, the market for it, the marketing of it, and its financial feasibility. "If you build it, they will come" made great cinema but it makes for horrible business advice. Pat's exercises for testing the market for your idea remove the guesswork and set your course based on data instead of intuition.

Will It Fly? is practical. It's simple. And I believe—after almost eight years researching *The ONE Thing* and then coaching individuals and businesses on those principals—it's your number one priority. Entrepreneurship doesn't come with a parachute. Make your first investment in your big idea be a few hours with this book. Complete the exercises. Think it through. The best way to ensure your success is right in your hands.

So place your seat trays in the upright position...it's time to see if your big idea will fly.

- -

JAY PAPASAN

Co-Author of the *New York Times* bestseller *The ONE Thing*

I

GROUNDED

When my son Keoni (kay-oh-nee) turned three, I couldn't wait any longer. It was time for me to teach him something that my dad passed on to me when I was a kid—a skill that I've gratefully kept with me all of these years. Like riding a bike, it's something you never forget once you learn how to do it.

I grabbed a sheet of 8.5" x 11" paper, turned to my son and said, "Do you want to make a paper airplane?"

I remember my dad and I throwing paper planes all over the house when I was growing up. There must be more than 1,000 decommissioned planes in my own personal history of paper airplane construction. All kinds, too: pointy planes, fat planes, huge ones, tiny ones, planes that flew straight, and others that did loops in mid-air.

And here I was, about to give my own son his first glorious taste of printer-paper-made aerodynamics.

Keoni looked confused by my suggestion. He asked me, "Daddy, how can you make a piece of paper fly?"

"Well bud," I replied, "you just have to fold it a certain way. Watch…"

I put a crease down the middle of the page, folded the top corners in so they met in the middle, and then folded the wings. As I held the finished glider with my right hand, I could see my son's eyes light up with excitement.

I pulled my arm back ready to throw and said, "You ready!?"

"Ready!"

"Okay here we go! Taking off in 10...9...8..."

I learned to stretch moments like this as long as humanly possible. My dad taught me that one, too.

"7...6...5..."

Keoni was trembling. He couldn't wait any longer!

"4...3...2...1¾...1½...1...0! Liftoff!"

I launched the plane across the living room and we both watched it sail smoothly over the vast ocean of carpet until it crashed into the window on the other end of the room and landed on the sill behind the couch.

It was a pretty epic flight, if I do say so myself.

"WHOAAAAAAA!" Keoni yelled. "I want to make one! I want to make one!"

Exactly the reaction I was hoping for.

I grabbed another sheet of printer paper and handed it to Keoni. Before I could give him any instruction, he was off to the races, folding and creasing like his life depended on it.

After about 30 seconds, he was finished and proudly displayed his new creation, holding it in both of his hands with his arms stretched out to me. I had to lean in to get a closer look because what I was staring at looked nothing like an airplane. It looked more like that piece of paper you forgot you had at the bottom of your backpack.

I was surprised by which direction he thought was the front, but not surprised when, after a big windup, the contraption didn't fly at all. It only landed a couple of feet in front of him.

He picked it up to try again and threw it even harder this time. It had the exact same result: grounded.

Clearly frustrated, he turned toward me and said, "I don't like paper airplanes." He disappeared into the other room to go back to playing with his brand new Batman figurine.

✈

WINGS

Why do you think my son gave up so quickly?

Sure, he was only three years old and many kids at that age don't have much patience and react quickly to circumstances like this. When trying something new is met with failure the activity becomes a sort of threat to children, which is why the typical and immediate reaction is to go back to something familiar that makes them feel comfortable. That's why security blankets and "binkies" exist, and why Batman would never be lonely in our home.

So what was a father to do? I couldn't just let my son's paper plane-making career end like that! So, I recruited Keoni back for a second go-around and, as I always do when he's met with a challenge, I tried to get him to figure out the answers on his own by asking a lot of questions.

"Keoni," I said, "Why do you think your plane didn't fly like mine?"

"Your plane is better," he said.

"What about my plane was better?"

"I don't know," he replied.

I grabbed my plane from behind the couch and held it in

front of him. "What do you see on my plane that you think makes it fly?"

He scanned the plane. "Wings?"

"Wings! That's right!" I brought the plane closer to him. "How many wings can you count?"

He pointed and counted, "One. Two."

"Two wings. Right again! Have you ever made wings before?" I asked.

"No."

"Well then of course your plane didn't fly, you haven't learned how to make wings yet! Can I show you how to make wings so your plane can fly, too?"

He nodded yes.

I retrieved two more pieces of fresh printer paper and laid them flat on the coffee table.

"Follow what I do," I instructed.

Together, step-by-step, we folded our planes and after a few minutes (and with a little bit of help from daddy on some of the more complicated folds), we were ready for liftoff. His plane was a little rough around the edges, but it was still a vast improvement over version 1.0.

"You ready?" I asked him.

He looked at me and asked, "Is it really gonna fly?"

I was pretty confident it would. I mean, the simple dart design was almost foolproof and in my experience it had lots of room for error, but how could I know for sure? What if I said yes and then it didn't? This was a crucial moment, so I chose my words wisely.

"You did your best to give it everything it needs to fly. You've given it a chance, and now all we can do is throw it and see what happens."

He pulled his arm back, ready to throw.

"Nice and easy," I said. "A little higher."

He paused for few seconds to make some final and seemingly important adjustments, and then all of a sudden, without any countdown, he launched his arm forward.

The plane went airborne. It glided across the room until it crash-landed into the front of the couch a few seconds later.

It flew.

And the celebration was massive! High-fives all around as Keoni screamed at the top of his lungs and jumped up and down like he had just won the lottery. "Dad, can you BELIEVE it did that?!"

I smiled as I watched him celebrate. I knew this wasn't due to any sort of luck. It was because he finally slowed down and took some time to give his piece of paper the necessary folds it needed to fly.

YOUR UPCOMING FLIGHT

If you're reading this book, you're somebody who is very close to launching a project of your own and making it fly, too. I'm excited for you because you aren't just making paper airplanes, you're thinking of something much bigger that could change your life and the lives of others.

I'm here to help you engineer its wings.

I've launched several successful businesses in the past, starting in 2008 with a website dedicated to helping people pass the LEED exam, which is an exam in the architecture industry related to environmentally-friendly green building practices. It might not sound that exciting to you, but the resource I created has helped tens of thousands of people pass their exam, and it changed my life forever.

I used to be an aspiring architect. I graduated from UC Berkeley in 2005 with a B.A. in Architecture and landed a dream job immediately after college, working as a drafter in a well-known architecture firm in the Bay Area. I was ready to dedicate the rest of my life to architecture and was doing all I could to prove it. I became the youngest person in the firm to get promoted to Job Captain and everything was going according to plan—until it wasn't.

In June of 2008, I was told I was going to be let go. After some mild depression and moving back home with my parents, I ended up turning my knowledge about the incredibly difficult LEED exam into an online business selling study guides, classes, and practice exams for this test. Within a year, **GREENEXAMACADEMY.COM** generated over $200,000 in sales. Since then, I've built several other businesses and have earned a total of over $3.5 million online.

Today, I can't even imagine what life would be like if I hadn't been laid off and started my own business. The freedom that comes with being your own boss and having full control over your future is amazing, but for me it's not about the money or owning fancy cars (we have a Toyota Sienna, also known as a soccer mom van). It's not about sitting at the beach all day sipping piña coladas. I work, and when I do, I work smart, but I have something else in my life that's more motivating than anything else—my family.

I have a beautiful wife, April, and two amazing kids, Keoni and Kailani, and I count my blessings each and every day I have with them. I go with April to bring Keoni to school and pick him up each day. I go to Kai's dance class. I get to have lunch with April at home. I love to do all of these things, and I would not have had the same opportunity to enjoy them in my previous profession.

Because you're reading this book, I know you have dreams and aspirations, too. You have a why that's driving you to figure out how to make it all happen. You can visualize what it might be like on the other end, but the runway isn't very clear.

Perhaps you're overwhelmed from all of the information out there and don't know what your next steps should be, or maybe you fear wasting your time and money building something that might not work out for you. Maybe it's both. Whatever the case may be, don't make assumptions and rush into things the way my son rushed into his first attempt at folding a paper airplane. As Joel Barker says:

" *Speed is only useful if you're running in the right direction."*

And that's why I wrote this book—to help you build your wings, and visualize your flight path.

I want to make sure you're clear for takeoff first.

Does your idea have merit? Will it succeed in the market you're trying to serve, or will it just be a waste of time and resources? Is it a good idea for you and the life you want to live?

In other words, *will it fly?*

This book is here to help you find out.

✐

MY SON'S FAVORITE TV SHOW
AND WHAT IT TAUGHT ME ABOUT
CONFIDENCE

Since Keoni's first successful flight, he has created at least 100 other paper airplanes. I'm proud to see him try new designs and not worry about failure anymore. His planes don't always fly as expected, but he has learned that failing is a part of the process of building cool stuff, and I've shifted his thinking from "I can't" to "I haven't figured it out yet."

He's twice as old now, and it's clear to my wife and me that he has definitely adopted an engineer's mindset. He's always trying to understand how things work, and if you let him, he'll ask questions for days about things he doesn't understand until he gets it. In fact, his favorite shows to watch on TV are *How It's Made* and *MythBusters*.

I've especially enjoyed watching *MythBusters* with him. It's a show that has aired on the Discovery Channel for over a decade that uses the scientific method to put popular myths to the test to either confirm or completely bust them.

For example, an episode that aired in 2004 tested the myth that a goldfish's memory lasts only three seconds. This myth was busted when the hosts Jamie Hyneman and Adam Savage were able to train a goldfish to recognize color patterns and complete an underwater obstacle course, even a month after it was initially taught.

Other experiments go much bigger, like the myth that a person can reduce their chance of being attacked by a shark by playing dead (confirmed), or that a water heater, if poorly installed, could explode and shoot through the roof of a house like a rocket (also confirmed).

And then, there are the super practical experiments, like the myth that talking to someone on the phone "hands-free" while driving is safer than actually holding the phone in your hand (totally busted), or that seasickness can be cured by taking a ginger pill (confirmed).

Okay, so I know I geek out about *MythBusters* quite a bit, and I know what some of you are wondering. How is any of this relevant? What's the point?

The point is our ideas are like these myths. We can assume outcomes one way or another, but until we put a method and data behind it to test those assumptions, we're risking being pulled into something that seems right, but may prove to be completely wrong. Experimentation will illuminate the truth.

Like they do on the show, you're going to take your big idea and scale it down into a controlled environment so you can understand exactly what's going on, and confidently make a decision one way or another.

LET'S TALK ABOUT YOUR IDEAS

You have an idea, or maybe a thousand. They could be new, or ones you've thought about for years. It could be a couple of words on the back of a napkin, or perhaps you've already crushed through dozens of spiral notebooks detailing exactly how it's all going to work and what it looks like.

When we get ideas, they possess us. They take up most of our brain space and it doesn't matter what we're doing—we could be taking a shower, driving, or even sleeping—out of nowhere our ideas can suddenly energize us like a bolt of lightning.

At the same time, it's much easier to keep ideas as ideas, because there is little consequence in imagining. Frank Lloyd Wright, a famous architect, said:

" *An idea is salvation by imagination."*

Good ideas are common, but those who are willing to take action and execute those ideas are far more rare.

Here are some reasons why one might just sit on an idea without taking action. See if any of the following resonates with you:

- ► You don't know where to start or what steps are required to turn that idea into a reality.

- ► You have a lot of ideas to choose from and you don't want to choose the wrong one.

- ► Your fear of failure outweighs your fear of not getting started.

- ► You're not sure if you're qualified.

- ► You don't want to let others down.

- ► You've discovered others who have executed a similar idea.

- ► You don't have the resources you need to get started.

- ► You're just not sure if it's going to work.

It doesn't matter how many of the above you connected with, from this point forward you must make a commitment to take action.

I can't predict everything that will happen in the future, but as John F. Kennedy once said:

" *There are risks and costs to action. But they are far less than the long range risks of comfortable inaction.*"

In other words, a sure-fire way to predict the future is to take no action at all. When you do nothing, you get nothing.

The following pages of this book are here to help you learn how to know whether or not that idea of yours is worth fighting for. You are going to spend a lot of time and effort on whatever it is you choose to do, so it's wise to invest a little bit of time upfront to put your idea through a series of litmus tests and thought experiments to give it the best chance of succeeding, or quickly get rid of it if it fails to pass.

This book is made up of a series of examinations. Not scary ones like you would take in school, where depending on how well you performed that day you are either smiling when you get your grade back, or putting your head down in shame. No.

You cannot fail these tests, because it's not you who is being tested. It is your ideas. No matter the outcome of the tests, it's always going to be a win for you. Either way, you'll have a clear indication of what to do next: go forth and conquer, or pull back and regroup to try again in a different way. If you go through the book and discover that your idea doesn't merit pursuit, you will have saved yourself a ton of time and money. If by the end of this you decide you've found something that works, you're going to be completely motivated to push forward with it, because you will have bolstered your confidence and busted your excuses.

Of course, in order for a business to become successful, it takes more than just coming up with the right idea. There's the execution of it, the design, the marketing, the copywriting, the offers, and so on, but none of those things will help if the idea isn't good. That's why it's insane to me that most people who teach business and entrepreneurship skip over this part.

Although I'm writing this book for you, I'm writing it with my younger self in mind too.

Even though I've created successful businesses over the years, I've had a number of complete failures too. When I look back and carefully examine each of these failures, the fatal flaw always comes down to one of two things:

1. Making money was more important to me than serving people.

2. I rushed into it.

Number 1 is a given. You just don't make money if you don't care about people first. Putting cash over caring has never rewarded me, and I've since learned that your earnings become a byproduct of how well you serve your audience.

And Number 2? Well, getting excited about something and rushing into it isn't a behavior that only children possess. It's common in all ages, and especially in those of us who embody the entrepreneurial spirit. Unfortunately, we don't just grow out of this nature. We have to learn our way out of it. I used to rush into things because I didn't want to waste time, but my haste often cost me *more* time (and a lot of money) in the process.

In 2010, I spent over $15,000 building software that never made it to market. I hired a developer before my idea was even fully fleshed out, way too early in the process. The consequences were a ton of miscommunication, wasted money, lots of stress and software that didn't even deserve a "good try." One of many expensive lessons learned, and that's okay.

I've learned that failure is a part of the process of becoming a successful entrepreneur. Yes, we have to pull the trigger or "just ship" as we often hear, but at the same time common sense tells us that a little bit of time up front to validate an idea can make all the difference in the world.

Can you imagine picking an idea and working on it for years, only to realize that it will never fly? How depressing and demotivating would that be? This book is here to stop you from saying to yourself down the road, "I wish I would have known..."

⌦

YOUR FLIGHT PLAN

This book is divided into five different sections, each of which is here to help guide you through the validation of your next business idea. This is your flight plan, and where we're going to make sure that conditions are ideal for a successful launch.

Part 1 is Mission Design, and it's the most important phase of this book. Through a series of thought experiments, we'll make sure your target idea aligns with and supports your target goals.

NASA has never launched a mission just because it "sounded like a good idea," and neither should you. There's a very specific purpose behind each and every launch, and a lot of time is spent planning and considering how each newly proposed idea fits into their overall plan, purpose and mission. Although you're not flying to the Moon or Mars, you will be putting a lot of time, effort and potentially money into what you're about to do, and if you discover that your business idea does not fit into your overall mission, then it's very easy to make a decision to not move forward with it.

A successful entrepreneur is one who is both successful in business and in life. Too often, I come across successful business owners who are still unhappy because their business decisions have not supported the life they want. The self-examination you'll do in this section will help you locate early warning signs so this does not happen.

In Part 2, we'll be going into the Development Lab to uncover important details about your target idea that you haven't even thought about yet. No matter how far along you are, we need to explore these thoughts in your brain and organize them into something cohesive and shareable.

We need to define your idea.

Through the exercises in this part, you'll begin to see what it might look like, how it will feel and what about it makes it unique. Afterwards, you'll have a lot more clarity about what it is you're really getting into, and therefore have a better understanding of what direction to take from there.

Part 3 is the Flight Planning stage. This is where you're going to assess the current conditions of the market that you're entering so that you can see what (and who) you're up against.

Although you might worry that you're "late to the party," the fact is that you have a great advantage over everyone else who is already there. You'll get a big-picture look at how your target market is being served, what's missing, or what opportunities exist. From there, you can favorably position yourself to win.

We'll be keeping track of the various locations your target market resides, we'll discover the top players in the niche and figure out what products and services are already available to them. We'll also conduct a few exercises to find out the true pains and struggles your target customers are going through, so you can come in and serve them better than they already are.

A lot of people skip this part of the process and try to wedge their way into a space they don't know anything about. Your Flight Planning will give you a huge advantage, even from Day 1, so you can properly enter a space with confidence.

In Part 4, you're going to enter the Flight Simulator where you will be combining everything you've learned through your research together to actually validate and test your idea with a small segment of your target market.

The problem that a lot of startups and entrepreneurs run into, even when they do the proper research, is that they don't validate the research through real-life testing with real-life customers. To really know if this is going to work, you need more than just *interest*, you need a transaction, and for many business models that means literally collecting payments or pre-orders from your prospective customers, even before you build out your product or start your service.

It might seem ludicrous to think that you can get paid for something you haven't even created yet, but when you can understand your target market well enough, truly define the problems they're going through, and become the point person who will provide that solution for them, it becomes a completely real opportunity.

And lastly, in Part 5, All Systems Go, we're going to do some final analysis to make sure you're ready to move forward with your idea. In addition to that, you'll get some helpful insight on your next moves, and how you can take a lot of the information you've uncovered during your research in this book forward with you, so you know your next steps.

And before we get going, I'd just like to say thank you. Not just for reading this book, but for being smart about your approach with your business. The world needs you. It needs your energy and what you have to offer, so let's work together to make sure you dedicate that time and energy to something that matters—both to the world, and to you.

PART 1
MISSION
DESIGN

" **Vision without action is a daydream. Action without vision is a nightmare.**"

—JAPANESE PROVERB

01

BEFORE YOUR
JOURNEY BEGINS

A few years ago, I received an email from someone named James, a long time fan and listener of my podcast. I get a lot of emails from fans, but this one had an eye-catching subject line:

SUBJECT: *I make $20,000 per month and I'm not happy.*

Hi Pat, I'm sorry to email you like this, but I had no one else to turn to. I feel like I know you because I listen to your voice all day. You're like a friend, even though we've never met. Sorry if that sounds weird.

Anyway, I want to thank you. You don't know this, but you've taught me so much about how to build a successful online business. I currently generate over $20k per month in recurring revenue, but here's the thing...

I'm unfulfilled. I'm not as happy as I thought I would be.

A few years ago, before I started my company, the thought of making this kind of money online was a pipedream. Now that my "dream" has come true, I realize that I didn't give my dream much thought at all and there's much more to life than just making money.

I don't even know why I'm emailing this to you, Pat. Maybe just to get it off my chest and share it with someone who might understand because you seem to have it all figured out. I don't know. I just opened my email and started typing, which is funny now that I think about it because I jumped into it without a plan, sort of like how I started my business. Clearly I need to work on that.

Anyway, I don't expect a reply because I know you're busy. Thank you Pat, for all you do.

— JAMES

I often travel to speak at conferences and, after the presentations are over and the last drinks are served at the sponsored networking parties, I traditionally find myself hanging out with a group of entrepreneurs at the hotel bar to extend the evening and talk business. Business conversations turn into life conversations, and over the years I've learned that James' situation as a successful but unfulfilled business owner isn't all that uncommon.

"How's life?" someone usually ends up asking, and if the answer isn't something on the same level as "Freaking amazing!" I always feel the need to dig deeper. I don't probe to be rude or disrespectful, I do it because I'm curious and genuinely care about these people. I wouldn't be hanging out with them if I didn't.

When you choose to live the life of an entrepreneur, you choose a path of freedom. You choose to live life on your own terms and can shape it into whatever you want it to be. In fact, everyone is capable of this freedom, but it is the entrepreneur who has mentally turned off autopilot and has taken control of his or her own future. This is why, when I hear about an entrepreneur who is unhappy in life, it makes me wonder how they have arrived there in the first place.

There is a difference, however, between being unhappy with life, and being in a momentary state of unhappiness with business. Building a successful business is an up-and-down-and-then-up-again journey that involves a constant shower of trial, challenges, error and failure. It is through these failures that we learn, grow and course-correct in order to build something successful and meaningful. Failing means we missed the mark, but it doesn't ever mean we're done. It simply means that we've come to a new starting point. Although failures are something we should obviously work to avoid, the reality is that they will happen. Building a business isn't always going to be sunshine and rainbows. There will be dark and stormy days too, but knowing that they are a part of the journey allows us to enjoy the process and incorporate the struggles of our business into a life that we can enjoy.

Building a successful business, however, is not synonymous to building a successful life. As entrepreneurship becomes more and more popular and is seen as the "cool" thing to do, more people are leaving their current occupations to start a better life without thinking about what that better life might actually look like. Not all businesses are created equal, and not all ideas should be built by the people who dream them up. It's when your idea supports your lifestyle goals that it becomes worth exploring more.

The purpose of Mission Design is to help you understand what your goals are in all areas of your life and help you determine whether or not your target idea supports them. How your target idea will perform in the market means nothing if you can't validate how it can support *you* first.

Skipping over this section is why people like James feel the way they do even after they've found success. Building a successful business takes a lot of time, so why should you spend it on something you could ultimately regret even if it were to become successful?

You might be thinking that this is a completely selfish way to approach building a business. After all, aren't businesses a solution to someone else's pain or problem? If we end up ditching that idea because it "doesn't fit into our life goals," isn't that greedy and self-centered?

The truth is if you don't have a passion for what you are doing, your energy will eventually fizzle out. It always does. By understanding your goals and the reason why you do what you do, knowing that your target idea supports your why, will motivate you more; and most importantly it will keep you going when times get tough during your business journey.

Plus, we're not getting into the micro-details of your business just yet. At this point, you probably don't even know everything that's involved with it, which is okay because I'll help you figure all of that out later. What we're looking for are the red flags, the obvious disconnections between your idea, and who you want to become.

Mission Design is made up of several thought experiments and exercises that will help you think about your future and how your idea supports or invalidates the life you want. After taking these tests, you may find that your idea fully supports your desired future self, in which case you can move onto the next section of the book to learn more. If you do find that your idea isn't one that matches the future you want, well then you'll be glad you figured it out now, as opposed to years down the road. If that's the case, start over with another idea, and then proceed like you did before.

Each test is quick and to-the-point so as not to waste your time, and you can easily breeze through each of these tests one by one.

Some exercises in this book may require you to write things down. To help you, I've created a free *Will It Fly Companion Course* that you can use to download worksheets and templates that are mentioned and utilized throughout this book. I've also included some bonus videos for you to help guide you even further along the way. To get free access to the *Companion Course*, which I do recommend you use while you read this book, go to:

WILLITFLYBOOK.COM/COURSE

I hope you're ready to dive right in, because our first experiment begins on the next page.

02

THE AIRPORT TEST

Welcome to your first test, a thought experiment I like to call The Airport Test. This test, and all other tests in this book are not worth being nervous about because there are no wrong answers and you cannot fail. No matter what the outcome is, it will be a win for you because you will have a better understanding of why you do what you do, and where your business idea fits into your life.

As with all of these thought experiments, they are meant to put a particular lesson into context for you, and in order for you to get the best results I need you to have an open mind. So let's begin…

Let's say you've climbed into a DeLorean time machine and zapped yourself five years into the future. You find yourself at the airport. As you sit in the terminal, waiting for your next flight, you feel someone tap your shoulder. You turn around and your face immediately breaks into a huge smile as you recognize an old friend from school. Your friend exclaims, "I thought that was you! It's been too long since we've connected!"

"Yes," you agree whole-heartedly. "I've missed you!"

With some time to kill before each of your flights, you both decide to catch up over a cup of coffee. As you settle into a table, your friend asks you, "So how's everything going? How is life treating you these days?"

You respond with, "AMAZING! Life couldn't get any better." And you really mean it.

Now here comes the key question:

What's happening in your life five years from now that makes you respond like this?

Don't even worry about the business idea in your head right now. Just fast forward into the future and really think about what would make your life, and all of the things that matter most to you, truly amazing at that point.

I'll help you think through this, but first let's talk about where this exercise comes from and why it's so important.

This thought experiment, as well as the one you'll find in the next chapter, is an exercise adapted from part of the hiring process within Keller Williams Realty Inc., the #1 franchise real estate company in the world. The company's founder, Gary Keller, and his VP of Publishing, Jay Papasan, co-authored one of my all-time favorite books, *The ONE Thing*. It was through a conversation I had with Jay that I learned the details behind this exercise and why it is so important to the hiring process within Keller Williams Inc.

When conducting this exercise with a potential hire, the company is actually interviewing itself on behalf of the person being interviewed. In other words, it's a way to make sure Keller Williams can support the vision and goals of a prospective employee. If the person envisions an ideal future that the company cannot support or doesn't fit into, then it's easy to say no. It becomes a win for both parties, because any future misalignments are discovered ahead of time.

While Jay was describing the process to me, he said, "If you put something up there that makes your life awesome that's not achievable with this job, it's my duty to say 'no' to you right now."

It's a unique, counter-intuitive twist to the hiring process. Usually companies hire a person because of the skills they can bring to a current position that needs to be filled right now. With the ideal future of the applicant revealed, however, a company can easily see if it's a good marriage. If it's a match, both parties will be more confident and happy to serve and support each other toward a common future. If it's not match, then both parties can confidently go their separate ways and avoid the monetary and time-based costs that come along with a divorce.

We can use this same exercise to discover whether or not your target idea aligns with your own ideal future. Think of it as interviewing your future self to make sure that you're making the right decision now, whether or not you move forward with this idea.

Entrepreneurs are notorious for "idea churn"—starting something new, only to abandon it for another idea. Sometimes this churn is fast, and sometimes it's slow, but our goal here is to reduce the chances of churn happening at all.

WHY FIVE YEARS?

It's also important to consider why we're talking specifically about five years into the future, and not just one or perhaps ten or more.

Five years is quite a long time, but not too long. It's about as far as anybody can reasonably project into the future with an executable plan to reach certain milestones and goals, but it's not so far into the future that ideas go beyond the capability of immediate action.

When you were into your second or third year of high school, for example, you may have started to think about what life would be like in college. As a high school student, you could potentially imagine which college you'd like to attend, what your major might be, and what activities you may participate in. Although college was still years away, you could plan accordingly and take the action necessary to achieve your goals. At that point in your life, however, it was hard to envision exactly what life would be like *after* college because it was so far into the future and so many life-altering things could happen in that time.

On the other hand, thinking about life only a year into the future has its own drawbacks. For some goals, thinking a year ahead is a perfect strategy because we can easily break down those 365 days into monthly or weekly achievements. However, it can also potentially hinder our big vision, as we get boxed into thinking about our short-term goals and only what's achievable within a year.

This is why five-year plans are so popular and why this particular exercise is vital for you right now. We're going to figure out what your five-year plan is and how your target idea fits into it, if at all. If it doesn't, then you don't change your plan, you change your idea.

Sure, I could have just asked you to go the traditional route and write down what you'd like to achieve within five years from now, but A) that's boring, and B) placing it into real life context makes it more meaningful. It puts real emotion into your search for an answer, and as a result, you'll think more deeply and honestly about how you respond.

Now that you know why this is important, let's get back to our little thought experiment and pick up right where we left off at the airport terminal coffee shop, five years from now:

"AMAZING! Life couldn't get any better."

And of course, like any good friend would, they react with a huge smile and say, "That's so great, I'm so happy for you! Please, tell me more! What's going on that's so great right now?"

To help you think this through, I have a small exercise for you to complete, and we're going to do it together.

-------------------------- **Exercise** --------------------------

Before we get into the technical details of what your idea is and how it fits in the target market you're trying to enter, we have to first understand how this potential idea fits you. Who are you and what do you want? What are your goals and ambitions? What's important to you? All of this is vital to define *now* before you proceed, because what you learn about yourself is going to guide all of your future decisions.

Investing your time, energy, and money into your idea without this knowledge is like piloting a plane without knowing where you're going. You either never take off, or you get airborne but eventually run out of gas and end up on the ground again, potentially farther away from where you want to be.

Let's begin.

STEP 1: Set Up Your Sheet

Print out the worksheet for Chapter 2: The Airport Test located in the free *Will It Fly?* bonus materials section online at:

WILLITFLYBOOK.COM/COURSE

If for whatever reason you cannot access the bonus material at this point in time, don't worry. Just grab a sheet of paper, and fold it in half in both directions so that after you unfold it you have it divided into four quadrants. It's important that you use a sheet of paper, because we'll be doing something with it later on.

STEP 2: Define The Four Most Important Categories of Your Life

Each of these four spaces on your sheet of paper is going to represent a category of your life that you feel is most important to you. You have complete freedom here and can choose anything you wish.

As I said before, we're going to do this exercise together, so here are the four categories of my life that are the most important to me:

- ► Family

- ► Professional

- ► Finances

- ► Health

You might have some of the same categories as I do, and you might have some that are completely different. Perhaps travel is a major category for you, or maybe athletics or music. Again, these are your own categories, so take some time to think about what best represents you and your future self.

After you come up with these four categories, write them down on your sheet of paper, each at the top of one of the four quadrants.

FAMILY 👤👤👤👤

PROFESSIONAL

FINANCES →

HEALTH

STEP 3: Determine Why Life is Awesome Five Years from Now

Now comes the fun part! Within each of these categories of your life, you're going to write down as many examples of things that would be happening in that area of your life five years from now to make you say that life is amazing.

Don't think of these items as "wish list" items or dreams. Don't worry about what it might take to get there, either. In this thought experiment, what you write down **is what your reality will be five years from now.**

If you get stuck, try to imagine your friend asking you, "What else is going on related to that?" And keep adding to your list until you cannot add anymore. There is no particular order you need to worry about, just write down anything that is making your future life amazing.

As you go through this exercise, focus on one section at a time. Because I'm doing this right alongside you, here is what I have written down for my first quadrant, FAMILY:

- ► April and I are 11 years into our marriage and we are still madly in love with each other.

- ► I get to go to school with April to drop off and pick up our kids each day.

- ► The kids are healthy, happy, and actively wanting to learn on their own.

- ► I cook and we have dinner together as a family almost every day of the week.

► Every couple of months we go on a vacation, small
ones during the school year, and big ones during the
summer when school is out.

► We are all open and honest with each other, even when
we're upset.

► April and I trust the kids to make wise decisions that
promote a healthy and happy life.

► I'm 100% present with my family mentally when I am
with them physically.

► My kids are super interested in entrepreneurship and
learning about starting their own businesses, too.

Okay, now it's your turn. In your first quadrant, add as many
items as you can. They can be specific, or they can be general.
Again, this is completely up to you, but remember this isn't a
"goal sheet." This is what your ideal life is like five years from
now related to these categories.

After you've completed the first quadrant, move on to the
remaining quadrants and do the same exact exercise with the
other categories of your life until you've exhausted as much
paper as possible. I'll continue my part of the exercise below.

PROFESSIONAL:

► I continue to get paid as a keynote speaker. Once
a month I travel to different parts of the world to
speak to audiences big and small about business and
entrepreneurship.

- I have written several books, including a *New York Times* Bestseller.

- I'm an advisor for a dozen different companies and organizations that I love, whose products or services I enjoy using.

- I've founded a non-profit organization that helps teach kids the principles of entrepreneurship, while also creating strong bonds between those children and their parents.

- I continue to absolutely love every moment of what I do, including the challenging parts.

- I have a recurring monthly meet-up in downtown San Diego where anyone can come and join me for lunch. Together, we discuss entrepreneurship and I answer as many questions as possible.

- My schedule continues to be extremely flexible, and I can take any day off I'd like to spend time with the family or go on vacation.

- Every time I visit my mailbox, I get dozens of thank you letters from people I've helped.

- I continue to practice ethical marketing practices. I haven't gone down the dark side.

FINANCES:

- Our primary home is completely paid for and we have zero debt.

- We have three other investment properties that we use for rentals that are completely managed.

- We have taken care of our kids' college funds.

- Our retirement account contributions are being maxed out each year.

- We donate and contribute at least six-figures per year to organizations and charities we support.

- My wife and I never fight about anything related to finances.

- Our kids do not earn an allowance, but instead earn a commission by doing chores and illustrating good behavior.

- The kids understand that they lose money by contributing to a complaint jar every time they whine about something before trying to solve the problem first.

- We have an emergency fund that's relatively liquid and easy to access that could cover two years' expenses.

- We make wise financial decisions and never spend money just because we can.

- However, we never worry about splurging on the things we love to do and enjoy, especially related to travel with the family.

HEALTH:

- I am more energetic than ever!

- I feel strong and can keep up with the kids, especially when playing sports.

- I'm continuing to compete in triathlons and have even begun training for my first Ironman.

- I've completed my first full marathon.

- I'm also on a soccer team that plays weekly near where I live.

- I have a six pack (without having to suck it in and flex).

- I make healthy eating choices and I'm an example to my kids in that way, too.

- I meditate every single morning and have a clear, confident mind when I approach every single day.

- My wife and I have both become examples to our kids to inspire them to live healthy lifestyles.

- I am virtually stress-free, and happy!

Here's what my sheet of paper looks like after this exercise is complete. It doesn't have to be pretty—it just has to be you.

FAMILY 👪

- April & I are 11 years into our marriage & we are still madly in love w/ each other

- I get to go with April to school to drop off & pick up our kids each day.

- The kids are healthy, happy & actively wanting to learn on their own.

- I cook and we have a dinner together as a family almost every single day of the week

- Every couple of months we go on a vacation, small ones during the school year, and big ones during the summer when school is out

- We are all open & honest w/ each other, even when we are upset.

- April & I trust the kids to make wise decisions that promote a happy & healthy life

- I'm 100% present with my family mentally when I'm with them physically

- My kids are super interested in entrepreneurship & learning about starting their own businesses too.

PROFESSIONAL

- I continue to get paid as a k̲ once a month. I travel to different world to speak to audiences big & small & entrepreneurship

- I've written several books, including
- I'm an advisor for a dozen companies that I love & enjoy using myself

- I've founded a non-profit organizati̲ teach kids the principals of entrepreu̲ creating strong bonds between those their parents

- I continue to absolutely love ever̲ what I do, including the challenge̲

- I have a recurring monthly mee̲ San Diego where anyone can come & lunch while we all together discus̲ & answer as many questions as̲

- My schedule continues to be extremel̲ where I can take any day off I'd like to̲ w/ the family or go on vacation

- Everytime I visit my mail box, I get̲ thank you letters from people I've helped̲

- I continue to practice ethical market̲ I haven't gone to the dark side.

FINANCES

- Our primary home is fully paid for and we have zero debt

- We have 3 other investment properties that we use for rentals that are completely managed.

- Our kids college funds are taken care of.

- Our retirement account contributions are being ̲ out each year.

- We donate & contribute at least 6-figures/year to organizations & charities we support

- My wife and I never fight about anything related to finances

- Our kids do not earn an allowance, but instead earn a commission by doing chores & illustrating good behavior

- The kids understand that they lose money by contributing to a complaint jar everytime they whine about something before trying to solve the problem first

- We make an emergency fund that's relatively liquid & easy to access that could cover two years of expenses.

- We make wise financial decisions and never spend ̲ just because we can,

- However, we never worry about splurging on the things we love to do & enjoy, especially related to travel with the family

HEALTH

- I am more energetic than ever!

- I feel strong & can keep up with ̲ especially when playing sports

- I'm continuing to compete in tri̲ and have even begun training for ̲ Ironman.

- I've checked off finishing a full ma̲ my bucket list

- I'm also on a soccer team that ̲ here near where I live.

- I have a six-pack (without having ̲ and flex).

- I make healthy eating choices a̲ example to my kids in that way

- I meditate every single mornin̲ clear, confident mind when I̲ every single day.

- My wife and I both have bee̲ to our kids to inspire them ̲ healthy life styles.

- I am virtually stress free, and̲

After you've completed the Four Quadrants of You, examine everything you've written down. This piece of paper defines who you want to become and it will be the foundation for several decisions that you make from here on out. When I did this exercise for myself the first time, it opened my eyes to a lot of what I wasn't doing to get to where I wanted to be, and it was clear that I had to make some changes in specific parts of my life (especially in my health quadrant) to help me realize this future self. On the other hand, this exercise also validated a lot of what I was already doing and the path I want to travel, especially when it comes to my family.

When I've shared this exercise with others, it has even brought tears to some people's eyes, especially those who, after seeing it all on paper, realize they aren't living a life they want to live. The bright side is that this realization has happened now, as opposed to years from now, sometimes when it's already too late. That's the beauty of projecting five years into the future. You have time to make some crucial changes. With your destination in mind, you can now create a proper flight plan moving forward.

Whatever your reaction is to this exercise, I hope you hold on to this piece of paper, at least until the end of this section because I have one more special thing for you to do with it.

✈

BACK TO YOUR FUTURE

Consider the following question:

You now know about your future self. You've defined the most important areas of your life. And you know exactly how you want them to look. So how does the business idea you have in your head right now fit into your future self, if at all?

Unfortunately, we can't jump ahead into the future to see exactly what would happen if you choose to move forward with the current idea you have in mind. However, I'm willing to bet you have some notion of what it would be like if it were to become successful. The purpose of this question, and the secondary goal of this exercise, is to catch any red flags. We want to find out now if it's obvious that the idea you have in your head isn't one that makes sense for you and your future self.

Most people don't have enough information yet, which is why the rest of this book exists. There are a few more tests we'll run through and an entire ¾ of this book dedicated after this section to refining your idea, doing customer research and validating it with particular target market you've chosen. But for some people this thought experiment is exactly what they need at just the right time. It was for me.

You see, over the years as my business has continued to grow, and more people have learned about who I am, what I do, and what I teach, more and more attractive opportunities have come my way. There have been a lot of opportunities that on the surface seem like they would be crazy to pass on, but it's easy to say no when they don't fit into my vision of my future self. If my million-dollar idea is going to take me away from my kids at this point in their young lives, it's easy for me to pass.

At this point, you have a decision to make. You can either continue to move forward with the idea you have and keep reading further into this book or, if it's obvious it doesn't fit into who you want to become, you can start over with something else. Just remember that either way it's a win for you. Even if you dump your idea, from this point forward you will never start over from scratch because you have the Four Quadrants of You already figured out.

If you'd like to continue on to the next test, flip to the next chapter, and let's keep going. You're doing great!

03

THE HISTORY TEST

I n the previous test, we time traveled five years into the future to discover how your target idea might fit into your ideal lifestyle. In our second experiment, we're going to get back into our DeLorean time machine, but instead of heading toward the future, we're going to set our time circuits to the past.

How far into the past are we going? It depends. When did you get your first job?

This is a history test. Not the kind of history test you take to see if you know when the War of 1812 happened, thankfully. You won't be required to write any essays or memorize any famous speeches either. What you will be doing, however, is examining and learning from your own past so that you can create a better future. Isn't this why we study history in the first place?

After all, as the American writer Robert Penn Warren told us:

" History cannot give us a program for the future, but it can give us a fuller understanding of ourselves, and of our common humanity, so that we can better face the future."

In The History Test, you're going to trace all of the jobs, positions, and volunteer work that you've ever done. By creating a chronological roadmap of your past work experience, you'll be able to discover some very interesting patterns about who you are and what works best for you.

This is similar to crafting a resume in the sense that you'll be listing what you've done in the past, but traditional resumes are boring and just scrape the surface in helping us understand who we really are, which is the primary goal here. In this particular exercise, you're going to dig a lot deeper and learn about your strengths and weaknesses. You'll find out what kind of things you like and dislike, and where you seem to gravitate. Finally, you'll see how your target idea fits into your personality and how it aligns with the trajectory that you've already been mapping out for yourself over the years.

I'll help guide you along the way and, like before, I'll be taking this test right alongside you. Afterwards, I'll ask you some questions to help you analyze what you've written down so you can see how your target idea fits into your overall life story.

Before we begin, however, I need to tell you that if at first you find that your target idea does not seem to align well with your past, this doesn't necessarily mean that you should dump it. Why? Because you might be due for a change, and in all likelihood, that's exactly what you're looking for—something different.

For example, if you've worked in the retail sector your entire life, that doesn't mean you have to continue to work in the retail sector. I want you to use this exercise to help you discover what it is about your past experiences that allowed you to thrive and flourish so that you can take those traits with you and incorporate them into your target idea. You might find the skills you learned in a previous line of work will be perfectly suited to support it. Your history might also help define what that target idea actually becomes.

Again, there are no wrong answers here. You're learning about yourself and keeping an eye out for any obvious red flags. Whether you continue with your target idea or not, what you learn in this first section of the book will stay constant, so during the next go-around, you'll be able to put your new ideas to the test even faster.

-------------------------- Exercise --------------------------

Like in the previous experiment, we're going to write a few things down. If you haven't done so already, you can print out the worksheet for Chapter 3: The History Test located in the *Will It Fly Companion Course* at **WILLITFLYBOOK.COM/COURSE**. If you don't have access to that now, that's okay. Pull out a blank sheet of paper, and I'll give you instructions on how to proceed. As in the previous exercise, I'll be doing it with you.

STEP 1: The What

We are going to look at different experiences from our past to complete this test, but for now let's start with the first job you ever had. If you haven't had a job yet, start with anything that you were involved with that required you to consistently show up and contribute in one way or another.

If you're still a student, for example, maybe it's a particular club or sports team you've had experience with. Anything you're involved with will work, including what you currently do. Here is my first entry:

> **WHAT: Employee at Picnic People San Diego**

(FYI, Picnic People is a company that hosts corporate picnics for companies in the San Diego region.)

STEP 2: The When

Beneath your first entry, write down *when* you did that, like this:

> **WHEN: 1998-2000**

STEP 3: The Good

And now, the fun part! List three answers to the following question. If you aren't using the provided worksheet, write down the question first, followed by your answers.

> **WHAT DID YOU ENJOY ABOUT IT?:**
>
> 1. **I got to work with some of my friends.**
> 2. **My schedule was extremely flexible and I was able to choose the days I wanted to work.**
> 3. **I liked having the ability to make people smile and have fun.**

STEP 4: Your Favorite Memory

Next, write down your single favorite memory related to this. It can be as long or as short as you wish, just enough to remember the experience.

> **FAVORITE MEMORY: One time, at a large picnic with over 1,000 people. When I was in charge of the bouncy house, a kid came up to me crying. She had lost her parents. I asked a co-worker walking by to watch the kids in the bouncy house so I could find the girl's missing parents with her. After about 20 minutes, I found her mom who was super thankful because she was just as worried. After the picnic was over, the supervisor for the day pulled me aside and he thanked me for taking charge during that situation. The thing is, I never told my supervisor about it, the mother took the time to find him and tell him how thankful she was about what I had done.**

STEP 5: The Bad

Next, let's think about what you didn't like about what you were doing. As before, list three answers to the following question:

> **WHAT DID YOU NOT ENJOY ABOUT IT?**
>
> 1. I didn't like having to stand in one place the entire time.
> 2. We had to wear these ugly uniforms-a bright yellow shirt with super short green shorts.
> 3. I didn't like cleaning up after the hosted events were over.

STEP 6: Grade

And finally, based on the following scale, please rate this particular experience based on how much you enjoyed it:

- (A) Everything about it was perfect!
- (B) For the most part, it was very enjoyable.
- (C) It was okay.
- (D) Didn't really like it much.
- (F) A terrible experience.

> **GRADE: C**

I love sharing this exercise with others. When done in person, everyone I speak to ends up smiling and they always learn more about themselves in the process, even after looking back at just one experience. It's funny how we forget a lot of what we've done, and it's interesting how we go through the motions of life sometimes without even thinking about why we like or dislike something in our overall story. That's why this exercise is so powerful. By looking back we can begin to see the colors that together paint a picture of who we actually are.

Repeat this same process with at least two other life experiences. They can be other jobs, organizations you've been a part of, something you've strived to accomplish, or anything else you'd like to examine further. I'll finish my other two, and then you can finish yours.

WHAT: Student Director for the University of California Marching Band

WHEN: 2004-2005

WHAT DID YOU ENJOY ABOUT IT?

1. I truly enjoyed my role as a leader and having a lot of influence on what the band did and what we performed.
2. I made amazing connections with other important people at the University, such as the Chancellor and Athletic Director. One of those connections even helped me land my dream job after college.
3. I loved the performance aspect of what we were doing. Working on something like a field show, and then performing it in front of

---

upwards of 70,000 people on Saturday...it was a total rush.

WHAT DID YOU NOT ENJOY ABOUT IT?

1. I didn't enjoy having marching band and architecture studio in the same semester. I literally had no time for anything else.
2. I didn't like how people felt intimidated or scared to talk to me because I was in a leader-ship role, especially when things weren't going according to plan.
3. I didn't enjoy the lack of respect some organi-zations gave us because we were a student-run band, which to them made us seem like we were not professional.

FAVORITE MEMORY: This one time, at band camp ...just kidding. Actually, my favorite memory was during the first college football game I ever attended and marched in. Cal was hosting the Fighting Illini from the University of Illinois, and although we got crushed (17 to 44), I remember marching off the field after our pre-game show and hearing the entire student section—about 10,000 people—all yell "Cal Band Great!" in unison. I literally cried because I was so happy. Never had I been thanked and appreciated for performing on a field like that before.

GRADE: B

WHAT: **Employee at Architectural Firm**

WHEN: **2005-2008**

WHAT DID YOU ENJOY ABOUT IT?

1. I loved how much I learned. Every day I'd discover new things about the world of architecture, both in terms of design, but also project management and teamwork.
2. I enjoyed the process of architecture—putting a lot of work into something and seeing the results of that work in real life. Literally walking in and through it.
3. I loved hanging out with my co-workers. It was fun to peek over the cubicle divider and start a quick conversation about sports or hang out during lunch or after work and unwind with a friend.

WHAT DID YOU NOT ENJOY ABOUT IT?

1. I didn't like how when I received my paycheck every two weeks, I felt like I was worth more to the company than what I was being paid.
2. I didn't like how I wasn't any more thanked or recognized than someone else doing half as much work with half as much hustle as me.
3. I didn't have any say or influence. I felt I had great ideas, especially to improve workflow and productivity, but no one would listen to me.

FAVORITE MEMORY: I was on a business trip in Florida to meet with a regional director of Hilton Hotels, who we were designing a 48-story hotel tower for in Las Vegas. A number of my other higher-up team members were there, too. This was a high-profile client, and I was there to essentially take notes. During our meeting, the main guy from Hilton requested to see 3-D photorealistic renderings of the hotel rooms we were designing, which our firm had no experience creating before. After a long pause, I raised my hand to volunteer to be the one to create them and said I had some experience in 3-D rendering. After he found out who I was, the regional director told everyone in the room he liked my initiative, and looked forward to seeing the renderings in a few weeks. The thing is, I had never done any renderings like that before, but after volunteering I was more motivated than ever to learn. A trip to the bookstore and many late night shifts in a row at the office later, I became pretty adept with a program called VRay and had the renderings delivered on time to the client. Soon after that, in combination with passing the LEED exam, I was promoted.

GRADE: B

If you haven't finished your three experiences yet, go ahead and do that now. You are welcome to do more if you like, which is actually what a lot of people end up doing.

If you read through my timeline, it's highly likely that you can already begin to piece together what kind of work I like to do and, more importantly, what motivates me. In both the marching band and architecture life experiences, my ability to have influence on improving things was important to me. People are important to me, too, and in all three examples, I shared stories about how meaningful it was to be recognized for the work that I do.

When I compare what I liked from these experiences with what I do now, it lines up perfectly. As an entrepreneur, I'm in total control over the entire operation. One of my favorite things to do is to analyze how I work and find out where else I can optimize my results and streamline processes. Additionally, I'm conversing with people all the time through the connections I make with those who I interview on my podcast, as well as with my audience via email and through social media. I'm able to perform like I did in the marching band through my time speaking on stage, and more importantly, through the service I do for others, I'm getting recognition for the work that I do.

Lay out each of your experiences in chronological order so you can see them all at the same time.

Do you notice any patterns between them? Chronologically, was the overall score getting better, or getting worse over time? If you were to share this with a significant other or a friend, what do you think their first impression would be?

Below are three questions to ask yourself about what you see. There's no need to write down your responses this time, but give these particular questions good thought before coming up with an answer.

1. **What one or two things seem to motivate you the most about the work that you do?**

2. **How much is your answer to #1 reflected in what you do now?**

3. **How can your future business be shaped into one that allows you to enjoy your work and continue to stay motivated?**

Question #3, of course, is what we've been leading up to with this exercise. How does your business idea fit into the kind of work that you like to do, if at all? If you're like most people, this exercise will begin to help you think about the kind of work that's actually involved with the direction you're thinking of going, but beyond that, it helps you understand how you can set yourself up for success.

As I've mentioned before, building a business is not easy, and it never happens in a straight line. There are a ton of ups and downs, and many times our highest points come immediately after our lowest. It will test your endurance, and understanding what motivates you can be the difference between giving up and reaching that inflection point where things start to take off.

Like in the previous chapter, determine if there are any red flags—extreme misalignments between the kind of person you are, and the type of business you're looking to enter. In any case, use the information you learned about yourself moving forward and hopefully we can make sure that no matter what business you choose to build, it's in alignment with what works for you.

I know you're excited (and perhaps a bit anxious) about

getting into the experiments specifically related to your idea, and we'll get there, I promise. Later in this book you'll understand how to refine your idea, talk about it with others and potentially get paid for it too, even before you build it. Before we get to that, however, there is one more thought experiment about *you* and your idea that we need to investigate before moving forward, and it involves swimming with sharks.

04

THE SHARK BAIT TEST

Your third and final exercise here in Mission Design could prove to be the most important one of all. In terms of timeline, we're back in present day. Your target idea is still just an idea, although it may have already begun to mutate due to some of the previous experiments we've put it through. The reality is it's going to want to change and morph throughout the course of this entire book, and if it does, let it. This book is a guide to help you shape your idea into whatever it needs to be to give you the best chance to succeed with it, and in some cases, as we've discussed before, that could mean not moving forward with the idea at all.

In this final thought experiment, you suddenly find yourself walking down a brightly lit hallway. Your footsteps echo through the corridor as you move across the polished wood floor. In the distance, at the end of your pathway, are two large wooden doors. As you approach, you notice the walls on either side of you are lined with brightly lit, blue-tinted aquariums, and out of the corner of your eye a small shark swims by and catches your attention, as if to say "hello" (although it could just as well mean "goodbye"). As you step closer to the doors they suddenly part for your entrance into a much larger room, well-decorated but a bit dim, except for what is highlighted with spotlights at the center of the room—a panel of well-dressed people who have been patiently waiting for your arrival. From left to right, you recognize Mark Cuban, Daymond John, Barbara Corcoran, Kevin O'Leary, Lori Greiner, and Robert Herjavec. You are on the hit TV show *Shark Tank*.

Shark Tank is one of my all-time favorite TV shows. As a viewer, you become witness to entrepreneurs who pitch their business to a panel of investors, known as "The Sharks," who have the option to invest capital in exchange for a percentage of ownership in that company. Some people walk into the *Shark Tank* and pitch beautifully, walking out with cash and a new partner to help their business grow. For others, the pitch can quickly escalate into a bloodbath that becomes hard to watch.

Either way, it makes for great television, and after watching hundreds of different pitches over the past several years, I've learned a lot about what makes a great pitch and what doesn't—well, at least in terms of what works for a TV show with this kind of format.

At this moment in time, you're not quite ready to pitch your idea. We'll work on getting your idea "pitch-ready" in the next part of the book. For now, I've asked The Sharks for a favor on your behalf. They're willing to take a few moments during a break while they film next season to help you out.

(Truth be told, I have not had the pleasure of befriending any of The Sharks just yet. But remember, this is a thought experiment. Thought experiments are made-up scenarios we create to discover something meaningful and useful in real life. So for the purpose of this particular thought experiment, consider The Sharks as my friends.)

Over the years, as a viewer of the show and an entrepreneur

myself, I've learned that there's so much more to entrepreneurship than the products or services being offered and what they can do. I've witnessed plenty of entrepreneurs with great products get ripped apart, both on television and in real life. On the other hand, I've seen mediocre products perform well for a different reason. More important than the product is the person behind it. That's why even though the focus here at the beginning of the book has been on your target idea, these initial tests, deep down, have been all about you.

So as you stand motionless but alert, like a minnow in front of The Sharks, you notice the gentleman in the center of the room, billionaire entrepreneur and investor Kevin O'Leary press his fingers together, look you directly in the eyes and say, "You know, I could probably hire someone right now to do whatever it is you're thinking of doing. So why should I be interested in working with you? What makes you so special?"

Nice to meet you too, Kevin.

This is a harsh question to begin with, but it's absolutely necessary for you to answer, because if you can't, you'll get left behind, like I almost did.

In January of 2009, my LEED exam business was taking off, primarily because I was one of the only people online who had any information about it available. That month, I sold 563 copies of my study guide at a price of $29.99 each. These were digital copies too, so I didn't have to worry about printing, packaging or shipping. A PDF version of the study guide was sent automatically to customers immediately after purchase. Because of this, virtually all of the income was generated passively. It kept my profit margins above 95% and freed up time for me to create new products and focus on marketing. Not bad for a one-man operation! Combined with the advertising on my website, I earned a total of $19,400.37 that month. The next month, my earnings increased to $23,106.16.

Then, it happened. The United States Green Building Council (USGBC), the organization that created the LEED Green Building Rating System and administers the professional exam, published their own study guide. I was doomed.

Why would anyone want to buy my study guides when they could get one from the organization that literally writes the test questions? I didn't get a perfect score on the exam and I wasn't a professional teacher. I didn't even consider myself an expert. All I had was my own experience studying for and taking this exam. Expecting to see a dramatic drop in web traffic and sales, I ended up experiencing the exact opposite. After the USGBC came out with their own study guide, my web traffic increased and I ended up having a record month in sales. But why? I didn't understand, so I sent an email to my new customers to find out:

> *Pat here, author of the LEED AP Walkthrough. Thanks again for purchasing my study guide. I hope it has already proven to be helpful for you. Again, if you have any questions or concerns about it, please let me know.*
>
> *The purpose of this email is to ask you one simple question: how did you hear about my study guide? If you could let me know in a couple of days, that would be awesome. Thanks so much!*

–PAT FLYNN, LEED AP

I thought about asking, "Why did you purchase my guide instead of the one published by the USGBC?" But I presumed they didn't know about it, and I didn't want to risk having my customers ask for a refund once I told them. As the replies started coming in, I was very surprised: most of them already knew the other guide existed.

Here's one reply that I received from a customer:

> *Hey Pat! Thanks again for your book. I take my test in a couple of weeks and your book and practice exam recommendations have already proven to be extremely useful. I'm confident I'll be passing with flying colors. To answer your question, I actually found you last week after searching for LEED study guides in Google. I was going to get the USGBC guide but it was a bit pricey, so I searched for other options and found yours. I liked what I saw and the price was right, but more than that I just liked the fact that you're real. You're just a guy who took the exam who was where I'm at right now not too long ago. I figured you would have some insider information as a test taker yourself. Keep up the great work! I'll let you know how I do.*

-JP

This was truly a revelation for me. The USGBC's guide actually helped me, not hurt me. It started a trail to my own products and also became a point of reference for comparison with two components working heavily in my favor:

1. The price, and

2. The fact that there's a relatable person behind the product.

The pricing makes sense. I was able to charge much less than the USGBC because I had virtually no overhead costs and staff to worry about, but later on I learned that cheaper isn't always better. In fact, I actually raised the price of my products and in doing so, sold even more because the price can affect one's perceived value of a product. Go too cheap, and people might begin to think there's something wrong with that item. If you spot a Mercedes on the lot for $500.00, it really makes you wonder what's wrong with it.

The second point is even more important. When examining the language my customers used in their replies, it became evident that there was a human connection there. They were like emails coming from a friend. All of them used my name and, like in the example above, many of them said they would follow up with me, and most did. You just don't do that with companies that don't make you feel like there's a person you can relate to on the other end, and that's when I learned what my advantage was. I was someone who was just like them, who had first-handedly taken the exam, too. That was something the USGBC and other LEED education providers couldn't compete with, and it became my #1 differentiator. Soon, I started to add more of my own experience with the exam on the site, and as a result my sales continued to climb. And remember, this is all related to studying for the LEED exam, a niche that on the surface sounds completely boring and impersonal—but when a human element is added to it, you've got something people can connect with.

I don't think there's anyone who put it better than one of my best friends and accountability partners, Chris Ducker, author of *Virtual Freedom* and owner of **YOUPRENEUR.COM**:

" *Building a successful business is no longer about B2B or B2C. It's about P2P, those people-to-people relationships."*

The fact that I could (and often did) build a relationship with my customers was my unfair advantage over my biggest competitors.

That is why before we begin diving specifically into conducting market research and validating your target idea, we need to validate you and your connection to your target audience. It doesn't matter whether or not you plan on becoming a public face to your company, we have to learn what it is about *you* that you will bring and incorporate into your future business.

Back to Kevin O'Leary, who is still waiting on your answer.

" *You know, I could probably hire someone right now to do whatever it is you're thinking of doing. So why should I be interested in working with you? What makes you so special?"*

How would you respond to Kevin's question? It's very direct, but it's a question you need to know how to answer. Unfortunately, not everyone on the show knows how to respond, and it becomes very obvious very quickly. Some people start talking about how big the market is they're trying to get into, which usually has The Sharks rolling their eyes. They know the question is being avoided. Others talk about how unique their product is and there's nothing else like it, but that's not good enough either. Competitors can come into the space and create something similar at any moment.

When I share this thought experiment with other people in person, it's easy to see that it can be quite deflating for those who don't know how to answer. After I ran through this scenario with a friend, he looked at me, completely crestfallen, and said, "Well, I now want to crawl into a hole where I can quietly die from embarrassment for even having this thought. Great game, Pat!"

If you catch yourself feeling this way too, you're not alone. A lot of people with great ideas have crawled into holes and never come back out. If you want to succeed, you need to push through these feelings.

This resistance that you might be feeling, this doubt in your head, is actually a sign that you need to keep moving forward; that this is exactly what you're supposed to do. As Steven Pressfield, author of *The War of Art* describes:

> "Fear is good. Like self-doubt, fear is an indicator. Fear tells us what we have to do. Remember our rule of thumb: The more scared we are of a work or calling, the more sure we can be that we have to do it."

Many of life's most amazing moments are preceded by fear or self-doubt, and what you're feeling right now in your journey as an entrepreneur is no different, you just haven't reached the other side yet. But we're getting there, and you've got The Sharks to help you.

To come back to this scenario, what Kevin is really asking you is this:

What can you bring to the table that no one else can? **What is your unfair advantage?**

✈

TYPES OF UNFAIR ADVANTAGES

I was first introduced to the term "unfair advantage" by Lain Ehmann, my featured guest on SPI Podcast Session #37: How to Monetize a Hobby Niche. To date, her episode is one of the most popular success stories on the show because Lain shares exactly how she's now earning six-figures a year online in the scrapbooking niche. Yes. Scrapbooking.

She describes an unfair advantage as a skill or asset that you have that no one else has, or very few others might have in a specific niche. It's your competitive edge, and whatever that edge may be, it's your job to use it to your advantage as much as possible as you shape and create your business.

This is different from a Unique Selling Proposition, or USP, as we often hear about when starting a business. A USP is about the business itself and how it's different than the rest. Your unfair advantage, however, is about you. It's what you have that no one else has. It's your superpower, and it should absolutely be incorporated into any business with which you become involved.

Lain's unfair advantage was the people she knew in the scrapbooking niche. Her experience freelance writing for scrapbooking magazines put her in contact with some of the top people in the industry, and in true entrepreneurial fashion, she started an online event called True Scrap that brought all of these people together to teach live classes to paying attendees who watched virtually. Thousands of people have attended these events and have benefited from her ability to connect with the right people. Holy scrap!

Gary Vaynerchuk, CEO of VaynerMedia, is another person that comes to mind who has a very clear unfair advantage over others, a superpower that he was brought up with that he's incorporated into everything that he does. He has an unmatched ability to hustle like there's no tomorrow, and out-hustle everyone that stands in his way. Seriously, the guy works harder than anyone I know, and he loves every minute of it.

StillMotion is an entire company that comes to mind when I think of unfair advantages. They are an Emmy Award-winning filmmaking company from Portland, Oregon that I had the pleasure of working with on a documentary a few years ago. They are successful because they have an unrivaled talent for telling amazing stories. As they say on their about page on their website, "We don't make commercials. We don't sell your product. We tell stories that make the right audience fall in love with you."

I could go on and on about different people and companies and the superpowers they've injected into their business, but let's bring this back over to you and The Sharks. Kevin is being patient with you (which is unlike him, but hey—we're good buddies and he owes me this favor), but he's anxious to hear what you come up with.

Q. "What makes you so special?"

How would you answer that question right now?

If the answer is clear in your mind, great! You're way ahead of where most people are at this point because determining what your unfair advantages are isn't something that happens overnight.

If you're like most people, you're running through a list of possibilities in your head but none of them are jumping out to you. Don't worry, because that's perfectly natural. It's a little weird to come up with unfair advantages on our own sometimes. It took me six months to figure out what mine were when I started my LEED exam business—and remember it was my customers who told me the answer. Over time I've learned more and more about what my other unique abilities are, and each time I learned what they were by listening to others.

The best way to know what makes you unique is to hear it from someone else, which is why I recommend finishing off Part 1 with one final exercise, even if you already have an idea of what your unfair advantages are.

-------------------------- **Exercise** --------------------------

You're going to email 10 friends and colleagues and ask them to identify your superpowers.

This might sound a little crazy, but this is an exercise that I've heard Gary Vaynerchuk and several other entrepreneurs propose, because if you don't know what your strengths are, you'll never be able to harness them.

Sometimes these kinds of exercises can get quite heavy, especially when you begin to ask for weaknesses or a recount of times you may have disappointed someone. It can be very useful to know that kind of information, but for this exercise we're just going for the positive, and I have something to make it even easier for you to help you get the responses you're looking for.

Below, you'll find an email template that you're free to copy and use for yourself when you email your 10 people. I recommend adding your contacts into the BCC field in your email so that you only have to send it once, and when people reply only you get to see the answers.

This takes the pressure completely off of you and puts it on me, and allows you to easily explain in an honest way where this is all coming from. Where you see [Name], that's where you include your name, and where you see [him/her] or [he/she], select the one that makes sense for you.

Subject: *From Pat Flynn on Behalf of [Name]*

Hi! My name is Pat Flynn, author of Will It Fly?, *a book that [Name] is reading about business. Don't worry, I'm not trying to sell you my book and there are no links to it here in this email. I've asked [Name] to send this to you because [he/she] needs your help and trusts you to give [him/her] your honest opinion. This won't take more than a minute of your time.*

I challenged [Name] to discover a unique trait or skill that [he/she]'s really good at—to find a sort of "superpower" that [he/she] possesses that can be used to [his/her] advantage while building a business. The best way to know this information is to hear it from others, which is why I tasked [him/her] with emailing just a few select people.

If you could reply to this email with what you believe to be [his/her] "superpowers" or traits and characteristics that you believe to be unique to [Name], it would help him out tremendously. Only [Name] will see your reply. Not I or anyone else he has emailed will see what you've written.

*If you're not sure about this and want to make sure this is real, feel free to email me at **PAT@WILLITFLYBOOK.COM**. I'm here to help [Name], and I'm super thankful you are too!*

Cheers, and all the best!

–PAT FLYNN

- -

If you'd like to send these out individually and add your own personalized message for each person, or send an entirely different message altogether, feel free to do that. The point is to send these out and get a reply to help you figure out what makes you…you.

Individual answers will be interesting to see, but it's the commonalities between multiple emails that can truly reveal what makes you special.

I first learned about this exercise from my friend Greg Hickman from System.ly, who emailed me and asked the same question. I knew that my answers, along with everyone else he emailed, would be extremely useful for him, so immediately after I replied I sent the same email to some of my closest friends. The responses were indeed very close to what I thought they would be: personable and easy to get along with, and an ability to take complicated things and make them easy to understand.

To show you that you have nothing to worry about, and to continue participating in these exercises with you, as I was writing this section of the book I asked this question publicly on my Facebook Page. Here are the top comments:

Smart Passive Income with Pat Flynn

Published by Pat Flynn [?] · 22 hrs · 🌐

Quick question for those of you who know me pretty well, and thank you in advance for taking a moment to answer. If I asked you what you feel is a unique ability - perhaps a "superpower" that I possess, what would you say that superpower is?

15,496 people reached   **Boost Post**

👍 Like   💬 Comment   ↗ Share   ≋ Buffer

Siddaiah Thirupati, TonmoyParves, Matthew Robert Tims and   Top Comments ▾
48 others like this.

1 share

    Write a comment...   📷 ☺

 Ginny Gay As a long time listener to you podcasts, I'd say your ability to connect with your listeners, identify the essential, meaningful ideas that they would benefit from knowing & then effectively communicate those ideas to them.
Like · Reply · 👍 3 · 21 hrs

 Paul Ramondo Providing unbelievable, actionable, easy to follow, no ego, step by step real value that always makes me want more - to the point where I'm beyond happy to pay for it.

#cantwaitforyourbook
Like · Reply · 👍 3 · 22 hrs

Taavi Pertman Making difficult things seem easy with über clear and specific step by step guides.

It's not a superpower, but it's a useful skillset to have ☺
Like · Reply · 15 mins

 Mikel Billstrom I'll ignore your overall character for this question because you're a genuine man,... Your super power is taking very complicated things and breaking them down step by step, to the point anyone can understand. In my opinion
Like · Reply · 👍 1 · 22 hrs

 Guilherme Torres Zeitounlian Your superpower is explaining things in an easy, down-to-earth manner, without wrapping it up on formulas or theories.

Also, you share a lot about yourself, we all feel very close to you - even if we are in another hemisphere of the globe ☺
Like · Reply · 👍 2 · 18 hrs

You may or may not get the refined answer you're looking for as far as exactly what your unfair advantage may be, but at least this will give you a good head start as you continue into the next part of this book. Keep in mind that it's our unique abilities that help differentiate us from others, and will give us a stronger connection with those who we serve.

And what about The Sharks? Well, they'll always be there to hear you out, and they look forward to hearing more about how your idea progresses from this point forward. Maybe someday you'll actually get to pitch to them in person. Until then, keep this thought experiment in mind as you continually hone in on your unfair advantages and utilize them to serve others in this world.

Before we move into the next part of the book and start extrapolating that idea in your head to mold it into something real, we have one more chapter to go here in Mission Design, something fun that I think you're going to enjoy. It won't require any more writing, but it will require you to be a kid again.

FOLDING YOUR WINGS

As you work through the next parts of this book, and even as you continue onward into in your entrepreneurial journey, along the way you're going to forget why you're doing all of this. It's just a natural part of the process. But, if you struggle to remember why you're putting in the long hours upfront and why you chose to go down this path, then you're quickly going to lose motivation and come to a screeching halt. You must remind yourself, often, of your mission and what you're fighting for. It's tough though, because in order to succeed in business we need to narrow our focus on the next task that's in front of us, but in doing so we sometimes lose sight of the big picture.

I'm lucky because every time I step out of my home office my two little ones are there to remind me of my why. Every moment I have with them makes me more aware that I need to crush it the next time I get back into my office, and why I can't afford to waste time going down a YouTube rabbit hole or worrying about the fear that's trying to stop me when I'm pushing myself forward and trying something new.

A lot of people ask me how I'm able to get so much done. My answer is because my mission is clear. Why else would I do anything but that which supports my mission?

It doesn't matter what your mission is, what matters is that it's yours and you have something to remind you of it. Lucky for you, you already have something in your possession that can serve as this reminder—your Four Quadrants of You exercise from The Airport Test back in Chapter 2.

The sheet of paper that you created in that exercise represents your future and everything you are working towards. Instead of taping it to a wall next to your desk or folding it in half and stashing it into a drawer, I'd like to invite you to fold it into a paper airplane and keep it as a symbol of your why.

A plane symbolizes flight, movement and innovation. It also symbolizes freedom. In the air, without the constraint of road and terrain, you can choose to move in any direction you'd like. Plus, paper airplanes are cool and make for great office decor!

In Chapter 5: Folding Your Wings in the *Will It Fly* Companion Course I recorded a quick video for you showing you how to fold your paper airplane into a simple dart design, the same one I taught my son Keoni how to fold on his third birthday. It's effective and it will fly. You can choose to fold another kind if you wish.

If you have children or even a spouse or significant other nearby, I invite you to share the experience with them, too. When they ask you what all that writing is on your plane, tell them what it means. It'll spark their curiosity and put even more meaning behind it for you.

BONUS ✈ EXERCISE!

If you're on Twitter or Instagram, I'd love to see a video or picture of your plane, and if you're up to it, its first flight! Only if you're comfortable sharing it, of course.

Use the hashtag #WillitFly, and if you want to make sure I see it, also include my name, @patflynn, somewhere in your message.

I look forward to seeing you take flight, and feel free to click into the hashtag to see other people in the community take flight, too!

PART 2

DEVELOPMENT LAB

" I can give you a six-word formula for success: Think things through—then follow through."

—SIR WALTER SCOTT

06

BEFORE YOU PRINT YOUR BUSINESS CARD

One afternoon during my junior year of high school, I was sitting in the middle of AP Biology. My eyes were starting to glaze over as the teacher talked about gene expression in bean plants when I felt one of my best friends tap me on the back. As soon as our teacher turned to the board, I reached my hand back and felt him press something into my palm. A business card. It was a little odd because I had never been given a business card before, let alone by a friend the same age as me. After I took a closer look at what was printed on it, I was even more surprised. I had to bring it closer just to make sure my eyes weren't playing tricks on me. Sure enough, his name was on it.

I immediately lost all focus on genotypes and phenotypes. This was way more important! Two thoughts quickly entered my brain:

1. What in the world was he doing with his own business card? And,

2. Where in the world can I get one of my own?

Within the next week, I noticed a lot of other students began flashing their own business cards, too. They were usually white card stock with some fancy decorative clip art in the corner next to the person's name. Below that, a list of some of their interests or talents, a phone number, and if the person was *really cool*, it would also include their pager number. No joke, pagers were a big status symbol when I was in high school, and apparently so were these business cards.

And of course, because I wanted everything that the cool kids had, I soon had my own business card—complete with a pager number. Like the others, I spent several hours avoiding homework to design my perfect business card in Microsoft Word and printed it at home using card stock purchased at a local hobby shop. After failing to cut them perfectly apart with scissors, I brought my mint-condition uncut business cards to school and used a paper cutter in the office instead. I felt like a professional. I was 16 and I had my own business card.

I look back and think about this "business card" phenomenon that passed through my high school. It was so exciting but, like most high school trends, it lasted about six weeks and then I never heard about business cards again. And with good reason—business cards for high school kids are ridiculous! These cards served no real purpose because no one gave them out to anyone but their best friends (who, of course, already had their number). And what businesses were these cards representing, anyway?

You know that expression that says, "You have no business doing that"? Well, we literally had no business, period. These cards were simply a way for us to believe and feel like we had something *like* a business, without actually having a real business.

I rummaged through my closet while writing this chapter to see if I could find my old business card. Unfortunately, I couldn't. But when April, who went to the same high school as me, learned what I was looking for, she found a few that she collected from her own group of friends and handed them to me. I literally spent the next couple minutes laughing, mostly because she found them in less than a minute.

Pretty absurd, right? Well, we have to remember that I was in high school and teenagers do strange things sometimes. Unfortunately, people today are starting their own businesses in the same exact manner. Before an actual business exists, websites are popping up, logos are being designed, and yes, business cards are being printed. But instead of phone numbers and pagers, it's email addresses and social media usernames.

Logos, websites, and social media accounts matter, but not until the idea of your business is actually developed. It's not until you fully understand what your target idea does, whom it is for, and how it differs from other similar solutions that should you spend considerable amounts of time on the branding elements of that particular idea.

The reason most people start with these and not with a fully developed idea is because designing your own logo and building a website is fun. Interacting with people on social media is fun. You put the work in and you see what you've spent time building in a relatively short period of time. Getting from our seed idea to a detailed business model is not always fun, and definitely not easy or fast, so when things get tough or we come to a mental road-block, we always go back to what can give us an immediate result.

Besides the visuals and the social media accounts, there's one other thing that I've seen a countless number of people waste their time on during the beginning stages of their entrepreneurial journey—the name of their business. I've met some people with incredible business ideas who never get started because they cannot pick the perfect name. I totally get that, because our businesses are kind of like our babies. We give birth to them, nurture and care for them, lose sleep over them. Sometimes they throw up on us, and then other times you sit back and realize just how lucky you are to be blessed with it. You would never not name your baby, like you would never not name your business; however you have to realize that the longer you stress over the name, the longer it will take for you to actually have one out in the world serving its purpose.

Now, I will say that naming your project is extremely important. As Seth Godin says in his book, *Purple Cow*:

" *Giving something a name makes it more real."*

You need this to be very real in your mind in order for you to have the motivation to follow through, so give it a real name, but don't stress over it. It can always be changed, and there's a good chance that it will, especially after you learn more about what this idea will actually become, the customer it will serve and how it gets validated.

In all likelihood, you already have a name selected in your head—and that's totally okay. If that's the case, then great—refer to your project as that for now, but don't be married to it. Like I said, it may change after you flesh out your idea, which is exactly the purpose of this second section of the book.

Here in the Development Lab we will take your target idea through a series of exercises to help you fully understand exactly what it is. First, we'll be organizing all of the noise in your brain that surrounds your idea so that we can visually see everything you're working with. Then, like sculpting a brick of clay, we'll be molding it into something real. We'll be moving parts around and removing unnecessary material, starting with the overall shape and then getting more into the details until we have something worth sharing.

By the end of this section, you'll be able to clearly pitch your idea so that you can begin to get honest feedback about it and move into the next part of the book.

Put your safety glasses on, because we're about to get started.

GERMINATION

T his is the first of three exercises that you'll be conducting to get a full understanding of what your target idea actually is, and it all starts with seeing. The word *idea* is actually rooted in the Greek word *idein*, which means, "to see," so we're going to take all of those thoughts in your brain, every single light bulb moment you've had, and translate that into something visual. Once you can see, you can do.

To help you through this, we're going to create a mind map.

WHAT IS A MIND MAP?

Our brains are constantly working for us, but the brain's capacity is also very limited to consciously thinking about one thing at a time at any given moment. We don't always think about things in the order that we need them, either. Unless we record our thoughts, there's a good chance that we'll forget a lot of what we think about.

Mind mapping is a solution to this problem and every entrepreneur should learn this valuable technique. A mind map is simply a visual representation of our thoughts, and it's an extremely clever and useful way to organize those thoughts and discover important patterns and relationships. Items can be grouped together, hierarchies can emerge, and it's not unusual to finish this exercise with a total understanding of all that noise in your head.

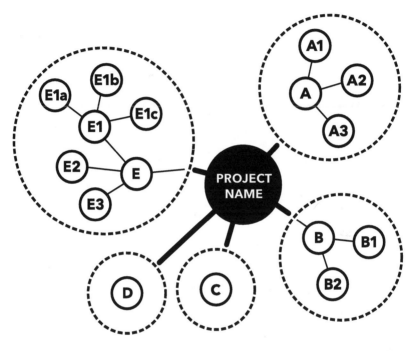

I've been using mind maps ever since I started my own business. I created one to develop my first online product (my study guide at **GREENEXAMACADEMY.COM**), and then later I started to incorporate mind maps into everything else that I did. I create mind maps for small things like individual blog posts and podcast episodes, and big things like new businesses that are built from scratch. And I'd be remiss not to mention that I'm using one to help me organize and write this book, too.

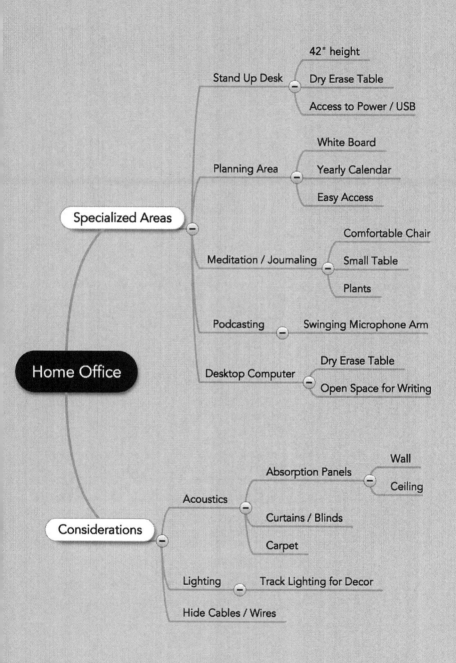

In order for mind mapping to work, you need to write or type your thoughts in a way that will allow you to easily move those individual thoughts around. A bubble diagram or list on a piece of paper won't work, and typing into a Word document won't do you any good. There are two methods that I recommend, one for fans of pen and paper, and the other for those who would prefer an electronic version.

METHOD 1: Post-it Notes

Although I started mind mapping with a computer, over time I've fallen in love with using Post-It notes to capture my thoughts and organize them instead. A single Post-It note represents a single thought, and they can be easily moved around, grouped together or discarded. Plus, they come in all different colors and sizes, which adds to the fun. I also like the feel of pen to paper, and when it's time to actually take action on certain items, I can easily pull a single Post-It note from that mind map, stick it onto my computer and keep focused on that one thing.

There are only two main concerns that come with using Post-It notes. First, Post-It note mind maps can take up quite a bit of space and you'll eventually want to remove it at some point. And second, Post-It notes are like kid magnets. To them, they're basically stickers. To combat both of these concerns and make sure you don't lose your work, just snap a photo of your mind map, and you're golden.

METHOD 2: Mind Mapping Software

If pen and Post-It notes aren't your thing (or you're worried about giggly pint-size Post-It note thieves), you can use one of the several web-based mind-mapping tools available to help you instead.

The one I prefer is called MindMeister, which you can find at **MINDMEISTER.COM**. You can create a few mind maps for free before you have to start paying, and they also have a great-looking interface so it's easy to use. You can also connect to your maps on the go with their mobile application, which has come in handy for me in the past.

There is a slight learning curve with MindMeister, however it shouldn't take you more than 5 minutes to begin to understand how to use it. The power comes in the drag and drop capabilities, which allow you to easily move your individual thoughts across the screen, or even group them together and create different levels and hierarchies. Plus, you can easily save your mind maps for later.

I hope you're excited, because in the next section you're going to create your mind map for your target idea. Before that, however, I have to give you the single most important rule you need to know to make mind mapping truly work for you.

Don't think.

Wait a second…isn't mind mapping all about capturing your thoughts? How are you supposed to capture thoughts unless you think?

Good question, but there's an even more interesting answer.

Without getting too psychological, your brain can be in one of two modes when you're creating something: create mode, or edit mode. Of course, there are more modes such as bored mode, frustrated mode or *a la mode*, but for the purpose of this example, you either create, or you edit.

Create mode is when you're imaginative, creative, and open to new ideas. Edit mode is when you are logical, regulated, and analytical. Most of us constantly switch back and forth between the two within a given piece of work, like when we write an email. You write a small part, read it, make edits, and then write some more.

The major issue is that your editor brain gets in the way of your creator brain. It stops the flow, which can remove the potential of amazing thoughts that you didn't even know exist in your head from ever coming out. You need these thoughts to surface during this experiment, but your editor brain can get in the way because it's too focused on making everything right or perfect. Thinking puts your editor brain into the driver's seat.

During the first phase of your mind mapping exercise, you need to be fully immersed in create mode. In other words, just let the ideas and thoughts spill out of your brain and flow onto your Post-It notes or through your keyboard onto your screen. The point is to capture any and all thoughts. There are no boundaries, and there are no stupid ideas.

Don't think.

In the second phase you'll be in edit mode, grouping thoughts together, removing what didn't work and finding order. In the first phase, just let it all out.

It's very much like writing the first draft of a book. The first draft is meant to be sloppy, but my favorite way to think about it was best described by *New York Times* bestselling author

Shannon Hale, who has written over 20 books. She once said, "I'm writing a first draft and reminding myself that I'm simply shoveling sand into a box so that later I can build castles."

Let's start shoveling some sand.

MIND MAPPING PHASE 1:
The Brain Dump

WHAT YOU'LL NEED:

► Your mind mapping method (Post-It notes or software) ready.

► A space where you'll be uninterrupted for 10 minutes.

► A countdown timer (like the one on your mobile phone) set for 10 minutes.

► Any other thing that helps you think best (e.g. coffee, music, your favorite chair)

► And finally, an open mind that won't think about order, structure, or editing.

WHAT TO DO (READ THESE INSTRUCTIONS FIRST):

When you're ready, start your countdown timer and then begin to rapidly write down or type as many thoughts or ideas related to your target idea as you can. Anything and everything is fair game. Do not edit, delete, remove, or move anything around yet.

If you're using Post-It notes, don't worry about where on your table, board or wall you stick your notes initially. Just lay them down and move to the next one. If you're using software, just create a new branch with each and every thought. It's going to get messy, and that's good. We'll clean it up in the next phase.

During this process, you'll experience rapid bursts of inspiration where your hands can't move fast enough for your brain, and other times you'll pause and look like you're staring into nothing. That's okay. No matter what, just keep going until your time is up.

Now that you're equipped and ready to go, have fun with this. In the famous words of Grand Moff Tarkin, "You may fire when ready."

As before, I'll be joining you through this process so you can see what it's like. Below you'll see the first pass of a mind map related to an online resource I built to help current and future food truck owners, which I called FoodTruckr.

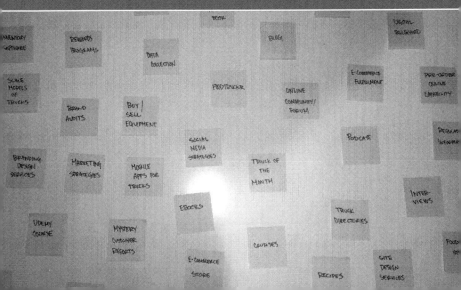

MIND MAPPING PHASE 2: The Clean Up

After your ten minutes are up, you might be staring at a sea of Post-It notes, or the digitalized equivalent of one. Great job! Here in Phase 2 we're going to turn on the *other* side of our brain and start to organize what we see. The overall mission is to organize everything you've written by forming visual clusters of your thoughts that seem to align with one another. To help you remember what those groups are as you go, you can use a different colored Post-It note or colored marker to designate that particular section. Or if you're using mind mapping software you can begin to name these groups by creating a new branch of your tree and dragging and dropping related thoughts in it.

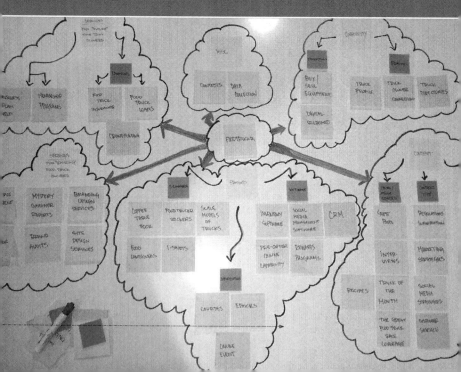

At this point, you're probably noticing some hierarchy and levels of your thoughts without even trying. That's great! You can start to order and create various levels within these clusters too.

Again, like before, there is no right way to do this. Go with it and feel free to be as analytical as you want. The more you think about why you're doing what you're doing, the deeper you can understand your target idea. With that said, if you have the urge to add another note or two to your cluster tree, you should do so. As you go through this exercise, gaping holes will become very apparent and you can fill them in as you go.

As you finish up, you'll find that there will be a few straggler thoughts that don't fit into any of the categories you've already created. That's totally normal and they are not bad ideas, they just deserve their own special straggler category for visualization purposes.

By the end of this exercise, your seed idea will have germinated and grown into its own lush tree, one with several extending branches and each branch its own set of leaflets.

Your target idea has structure; it's becoming real.

Take a good look at your mind map. That's everything that came across your brain related to your seed idea. Nicely done! We're not finished though, because if you were to incorporate everything you wrote into your business all at the same time, you'd be in big trouble. Smart entrepreneurs start by focusing on the essentials first.

So what do you do when you have a tree that is growing a little too wild?

You prune it.

MIND MAPPING PHASE 3:
Pruning Your Tree

More is not always better, and when it comes to entrepreneurship, more can mean disaster. Software, for example, is notorious for "feature creep," meaning it's easy to keep adding new features and capabilities. The feature creep dilutes the overall strength of the product, and as a consequence, the user experience is diminished.

Pruning is not an easy task. You just spent quite a bit of time creating your mind map, and now you have to remove some of those thoughts—and a few of them might be hard to let go. Remember, all you've done so far is shoveled a load of sand. Now you're going to start building your castle.

Start by removing the low hanging fruit—the obvious notes that don't really belong. Since your edit mode was off during your initial brainstorming session, you likely have a number of thoughts that just don't seem like they need to be there. Some may even make you say, "What was I thinking?!"

Don't stress if you find some notes that don't fit your idea. It's a sign that your creative brain was enabled, and that's a good thing! Take a few minutes to discard those notes that don't really matter.

What you have left in front of you is what you need in order to move forward. Should we prune some more? Absolutely. We just don't need to do right now. We'll be coming back to your mind map for a second round of pruning after we learn more about exactly who your target audience is and who else or what else is already serving them. We'll dive deep into that research in Part 3.

For now, take a moment to save the current state of your mind map and be proud of the work you've done so far. Even if you later find out the idea that you've mind mapped won't work, you have the skill to mind map anything else you'd like to organize from your brain in the future. You've taken a lot of action already but, of course, we're just getting started. In the next stage of the Development Lab, we'll be converting your entire mind map into something more tangible and cohesive: a single sentence.

ONE SENTENCE

When I was a drafter at an architecture firm, I worked under one of the top performing Studio Directors in the firm. Beyond his decades of experience in the industry, he was also a towering 6 feet 6 inches tall, muscular, and never took any B.S. from anyone. In other words, he scared the crap out of me.

He was actually the one who interviewed me before I was hired, and I vividly remember sitting timidly in the chair across his desk, thinking to myself, "If I get hired, I hope I don't end up working for this guy directly." Then he hired me for his department. As scary as he was, he taught me a lot about architecture and, more importantly, he taught me a lot about communication.

You see he was a busy man who was always in demand. As Director of the restaurant division within the firm, he was always in a meeting, on a conference call, or eating something that looked super healthy. Sometimes it was all three at the same time thanks to the Bluetooth wireless headset that might as well have been surgically implanted into his ear. It looked like Terminator was walking through the halls of our building.

In what little free time he had between meetings, he would check up on the team to see how our projects were coming along. He'd start with the Project Managers who sat closest to his office (poor fellows), then the Job Captains, and then finally over to us Drafters. I don't know if it was because I was the new guy, or because my posture somewhat resembled an injured gazelle on the Serengeti, but he seemed to pick on me the most. Conversations with others would only last 30 to 45 seconds, but with me they lasted for several uncomfortable minutes.

One time, he came over to my desk and asked me, "Patrick, why are you taking twice as long as Ariana to finish your drawing set?" On another occasion, after watching over my shoulder for a few minutes, he asked me to get up, took my seat in front of everyone and proceeded to demonstrate how to run a certain kind of function in AutoCAD. He wasn't my favorite person in the world (and I was fairly certain the feeling was mutual). So when he called me into his office one afternoon, I felt like I was in for it.

"Patrick," he said, even though everyone else in the office called me Pat. "Do you know why I'm so hard on you?"

I was surprised he admitted this, but how was I supposed to answer? "Because you're a cyborg from the future?"

"I don't," I replied.

"I'm hard on you because I want you to succeed as an architect, and in order to succeed in this industry you have to learn fast, and implement faster. You're new, and I'm teaching you so you can catch up and keep up with the rest of the team. When I ask you a question, it's never out of disrespect. I just want the answer so that we can figure out a solution. I don't have time for anything else."

I started to see where he was coming from. When he asked me why I taking twice as long as my colleagues, he really wanted to know why so that he could find a way to fix it. When he watched me perform functions in AutoCAD that weren't done in the fastest and most efficient manner, there was no better way to teach me the right way than to sit down in my chair and show me.

Standing in his office, he then taught me something that changed every single encounter I had with him after that point:

"Whenever I ask you a question, Patrick—in an email, on the floor, or in my office—I want you to respond in just one sentence. That's all you get. Think about what you need to say in one sentence that will convey all of the necessary items that will help me understand exactly what's going on. One sentence. Nothing more. Do you understand?"

"Yes."

-------------------------- ▷ --------------------------

After that afternoon, communication with my boss was far more efficient. I learned to get to the core of whatever was being asked of me and this new method of communication began to affect my conversations with other people in the office too, in a good way. Slowly but surely, I became less of a production bottleneck and caught up with the rest of the team. Over time, I began to excel in the office and was soon promoted to Senior Drafter, and then later Job Captain—the youngest to have ever been promoted to that position in the history of the firm.

It was then that I started studying for the LEED exam, which is eventually what my first business was about after I was let go during the recession of 2008. Perhaps if it weren't for my boss's aggressive style of communication, I wouldn't be doing what I'm doing today.

Although I'm not doing architecture anymore, I did bring what I learned in the industry with me into the world of entrepreneurship. I learned about managing timelines for huge projects, some of which could take often several years to complete. I learned how to use Photoshop, which is what I use frequently to create a lot of the graphics that I sprinkle throughout my brand. But most importantly, I learned about communication and how important it is to get to the core of things.

When you get to the core, you find what really matters. In the following exercise, we're going to take what we've already created—our mind map—and convert all of those ideas and thoughts into a single sentence. By the time we're done with the exercise, we'll be able to convey the very core of our target idea in a single sentence.

This is the first time you'll be communicating the current state of your fleshed out idea with others, but it's not an elevator pitch, as you may have come to assume. An elevator pitch is important, but we're not trying to sell our idea at this point. We're simply *sharing* the target idea in a manner that's best to collect honest feedback from anyone. We'll talk about why it's important to talk about your business in the next section, but for now, let's conduct an exercise to help you figure out what you're going to say.

✈

YOUR ONE SENTENCE

If you were to show someone your mind map right now, assuming they already know what a mind map is, it's going to be very difficult for them to understand exactly what you're trying to create. They could interpret it and be close, but when you present your idea to others for feedback, you don't want to leave any room for misinterpretation. So, think of this as a translation exercise. You're going to translate your mind map into something that can be easily understood.

This exercise consists of writing three iterations of your target idea:

1. One page

2. One paragraph

3. One sentence

With each step you will be further refining your idea, distilling it down to the essential elements.

I heard about this exercise through one of my good friends, Jaime Tardy of **EVENTUALMILLIONAIRE.COM**. She and I have been meeting weekly for nearly five years in a small mastermind group where we all share ideas with each other and hold each other accountable for our work. In one meeting, I shared how I was struggling to discover the focus of my next book. I knew what I wanted it to be about but I couldn't articulate the true essence of what it would be. She gave me this exercise, and like a sniper, I was able to zoom in on the core message that I wanted to portray. And now, you're reading that very book.

Let's take a closer look at each step.

STEP 1: Write One Page

To help you zoom into your one sentence, you're going to start with a larger field of vision and write a one-page summary of your target idea. This will run about 400 to 500 words and will allow you to write with freedom and turn your mind map into something tangible. It doesn't have to be perfect, and don't worry about spelling or grammar. Just get started, and have fun with it.

STEP 2: Write One Paragraph

Next, you have the challenge of taking what you wrote in your single page and condensing it into a single paragraph, about 3-5 sentences in length. Keep it to that, and remember to focus on what the person on the other end might need to know in order to fully understand what your target idea is all about.

This isn't easy, and it shouldn't be, but by the end you'll have an appealing paragraph that you can use to describe your business in a quick conversation.

STEP 3: Write One Sentence

And now the final step. Take what you wrote in your paragraph and distill that into one single sentence. Not surprisingly, this step will likely take you the longest to complete even though it requires the least amount of writing. And if you're like most people, you'll pen several different versions before you finally land on one that you like.

Here's the one sentence I devised for what I thought FoodTruckr would become:

> *FoodTruckr is an online resource that provides quality content, a connected community, and support for everyone interested in starting and running a successful food truck business.*

Read your sentence out loud and listen to how it sounds. How does it feel? If it doesn't sound right or if you aren't super stoked about it, those you share it with will feel the same way. Keep making adjustments until you have a sentence you can confidently proclaim, because that's exactly what you're going to do in the next and final stage of the Development Lab.

09

CONVERSATION AND OBSERVATION

Early in the life of my podcast, I had the pleasure of interviewing John Saddington (John.do), a serial entrepreneur who has built and sold multiple businesses for well over seven figures each. He and I first met at a conference in Nashville in 2013 and we connected instantly, mainly due to the fact that we both were young entrepreneurial parents of abnormally hyperactive kids, and we loved every minute of it.

During the interview (Podcast #61), we started with a deep dive into his journey into entrepreneurship, but then quickly shifted the discussion to best practices and strategies for succeeding as an entrepreneur. Because he had several successful businesses under his belt, I wanted to know what his first steps were after he comes up with an idea for a new business. His answer was not what I had expected:

> *This is kind of a very global and very quick overview, but the first thing you do when you have a great idea is you write it down. You don't keep it in your brain. You write it down, you vomit as much as you possibly can on a physical piece of paper. I could spend a lot of time on why I think physical pieces of paper are really valuable. So don't just put it in Evernote, don't just put it on a text document on your computer.*

Actually write it down. There's something powerful when you apply pressure with the pen on the pieces of paper.

And then I want you to carry it around wherever you go for the next couple of weeks, or even the next month. I want you to share it with as many people as you possibly can. The people that you know, your spouse, your kids, your friends, maybe your business partners, people at Starbucks, in line at your local deli—EVERYONE. Because this is what happens when you start sharing that idea—it starts becoming refined. And a refined idea is a much more mature idea.

You'll get quick feedback—instant, guttural feedback from people—and especially from complete strangers that say 'that is a stupid idea' or 'that's a great idea but have you thought about this?' And again, because you have a piece of paper, you don't have your iPhone, it's harder to type on your iPhone, you can quickly add that. And so that's what I do with great ideas. I capture them and I start sharing it, because now the idea is refined."

As he was sharing this, my mind immediately went to where it probably is for you right now, and I took the very first chance I had to ask a clarifying question.

Q. What's stopping people from copying my idea?

And John's reply couldn't have been any more motivating:

" *Nothing. But, here's the difference between you and the next person on the street who has a great idea—if you're committed and you love the idea, you will actually see it to completion.*

Most people never execute on their ideas because they just never execute. The reason I'm a success as an entrepreneur, and why many other entrepreneurs are a success is simply because we do it. We don't just talk about it; we do it.

But talking about it is where it starts, and because when you start talking about it with other people, you continue to drive the motivation. You continue to build momentum, and you continue to get excited on a much better and much more refined idea. So after an incubation period—could be a week, could be two weeks, could be a month, you have a better idea about your great idea."

It was after this interview that I started to follow John's advice and share new ideas openly with other people. I had already been doing that on my blog, but I started to do it in public and in person, sometimes with complete strangers, and I can vouch for everything John said. The feedback, the questions and the interactions completely help to refine the ideas that are being discussed. In many instances, new and better ideas surfaced that I would have never discovered had I not had these worthwhile interactions.

FOOD FOR THOUGHT

A few months after this interview, I decided to start a new side business publicly on my blog, as I did once before. Through research that I openly shared, I landed on the idea of creating a resource for people who were interested in starting and running a food truck. I had recently become a fan of food trucks myself, and was curious about how the process worked. I searched for anything helpful that I could find on the Internet, but nothing came up. Then, it was through real life conversations that I had with friends, food truck owners, and even complete strangers that I refined that idea into what eventually became **FOODTRUCKR.COM**.

Everyone I spoke with thought it was a good idea because food trucks were starting to become massively popular at the time. Beyond that, everyone I talked to lit up when I asked him or her what kind of food truck they would create if they had the chance. That was a great sign. On the other hand, those same people inevitably asked me the same exact question, "So do you own a food truck of your own?"

I didn't.

And when the person who I was speaking with learned that truth, it became an instant credibility killer and the conversation immediately changed its tone. And quite appropriately too, because why would anyone take advice from someone with no credibility?

This is the kind of guttural, instinctive reaction John was talking about, and it's exactly what I needed to hear. If I had rushed into building a solution without ever considering this, I would have been doomed right from the start. These conversations taught me that I had to find a way to make the content within my resource (and its source: me) credible, and if I couldn't, then I had to step away from the idea.

The solution, however, was obvious to me. I always choose honesty, so it was easy for me to decide to be completely open about the fact that I didn't own a food truck of my own. As far as content, I decided to establish credibility through featuring the advice, stories, strategies, and tips learned from other food truck owners, both with written content on the blog, and interviews on the FoodTruckr School Podcast. I positioned myself as simply the curator of valuable information.

I took my refined idea to the streets of San Diego and had even more conversations with local food truck owners to see how they'd react. It was much, much better. While it would be ideal if I had experience in the industry beyond being a consumer, my honest approach made me more believable and earned me more respect. And it became obvious that learning about how other food truck owners were running their business was something that they all would love to have access to.

There was one conversation I had with a particular food truck owner that proved to be the most useful, however, and again it was a result of a doubt in that person's mind. After learning about my idea, she ended up asking me the following question:

" *What's stopping someone with experience **inside** this industry from doing exactly what you're planning to do?"*

It was a legit question, and quite honestly very deflating when I first heard it because I knew the answer was nothing. I didn't have a response for her so I diverted the conversation to other things, but after going home that night I couldn't help but constantly think about what she had said.

I was at a wall, but like all entrepreneurs should do, I began to look at this wall from different angles. I rephrased the question so that I could use it to my advantage:

" *What's something I can add that even someone with experience inside this industry couldn't do?"*

In other words, what was my unfair advantage in this space? You've already learned about your own unfair advantages during Mission Design earlier in this book, so I hope you're somehow incorporating those into your own descriptions of your business. For this particular situation, my unfair advantage became the extensive knowledge I have about online marketing and social media, something food truck owners know is important, but many lack a lot of the more advanced skills and strategies beyond the basics. Most food truck owners don't even have an email list! Differentiating myself as someone with such knowledge is something I do on **FOODTRUCKR.COM** quite often, mainly by just providing helpful solutions to this audience that clearly incorporate my unfair advantage.

FEEDBACK MATH

As you can see, small conversations about your business can help you refine your idea in a huge way. You need to do this—and I know you will. Before you start, however, I have a few more important things to share with you to make sure you get the most out of this exercise. Remember, this is the first time you'll be talking openly about your idea with others, so I completely understand if you're nervous. That's natural, but I won't lie to you and say this is going to be easy, especially if you're the type of person who doesn't take criticism and negative feedback very well.

When you put yourself out there, you open the floor for both positive and negative feedback, and if you're like most aspiring entrepreneurs, your feedback math might look a little like this:

1 negative comment > 100 positive comments.

I completely understand, because my math used to look like that too. Negative comments and criticisms would stick with me all day, and sometimes they'd be so harsh they would rock me to the core, especially when it came my way in a manner where respect was nowhere to be found.

It took me a while to learn this, but I'm glad to be able to pass this along to you now this early in your journey. If there is no respect found in someone's comment or response, then there is no need to pay them any attention.

Every second you waste thinking about a hater or troll is a second you're taking away from those who matter and can benefit from what you have to offer.

Negative feedback and criticism given in a respectful manner is often extremely useful. Just look at 1-star and 2-star reviews for various products on **AMAZON.COM**. If they are legitimate reviews, they can actually include a lot of helpful feedback that the product owner could take into consideration for improving that product and the overall customer experience.

Now, you're going to get negative feedback at some point in your entrepreneurial journey, and it'll likely come very soon. Expect it, because it's totally a part of the process and the ritual of becoming an entrepreneur. It's as if the world begins to test us to see if we're actually cut out for what we're trying to do. You are cut out for it, as long as you keep going.

With regard to this particular exercise (and always through-out your entrepreneurial career) you want that negative feedback because it's going to help you shape your idea into something great! Plus, this is great training for you in general, and the more you practice accepting feedback, both positive and negative, the better an entrepreneur you will become.

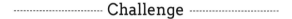

Challenge

Over the next two days, your challenge is to talk to 10 people about your target idea. I encourage you to speak to more, but 10 is a great starting point to cover a wide array of potential reactions.

Start with people you're comfortable with, who you know would care to listen and provide great feedback. Then try to speak to at least two people who you've never met before.

You've already put in the work to learn how to clearly and concisely articulate what your idea is, and you've even narrowed it down into just a single sentence. You have almost everything you need to get started. Below is a list of a few more tips to consider as you run through this exercise.

TIPS FOR HOW TO SHARE YOUR IDEA:

► DON'T GIVE ANY OPINIONS LEADING UP TO THE CONVERSATION. Never start with anything that sounds like, "I have the best idea for…" or "Do you want to hear a cool idea?" It's commonplace in casual conversation to start this way, however starting with "best" or "cool" or anything else

---

that frames how great your idea is could potentially backfire. Let the idea itself (and all you've done to refine it) do the work for you.

▶ **DON'T SELL YOURSELF (OR YOUR IDEA) SHORT.** One of my biggest pet peeves is when people start presentations by sharing how they didn't have enough time or it's not fully complete. If you start negatively, your idea will be perceived negatively. The same goes with your conversations here. You've put in a good amount of work so stop with the excuses, be confident in your approach, and know that this is all part of the process. You got this!

▶ **HELP. THEN ASK.** When sharing your idea with someone you've never met before, one of my favorite things to do is help him or her out first before I ask for help myself. For example, I'll buy coffee for the person behind me in line, which opens up the door for a quick conversation while we both wait for our coffee. When I lead into asking about my idea, I always ask first if they have time to answer a quick question. If not, then no worries. If they say yes, then I'll follow up with, "Thanks! This won't take more than a minute. I'm an entrepreneur who is looking for honest feedback about a potential business idea, and I love to ask random people what they think so I can get an initial reaction. Do you mind if I take one minute to share it with you?" You've already helped them out, so chances are they'll be more than happy to return the favor.

TIPS FOR HOW TO LISTEN:

► **CONSCIOUSLY LISTEN TO THE PERSON'S RESPONSE.** "Okay, Captain Obvious!" you might be thinking. However, consciously listening to feedback is actually a lot harder than it sounds. Your brain is going to fire up as you listen, and you might actually miss some important indicators along the way. I used to struggle during podcast interviews in the same way. I would be so worried about what my next question would be, I'd actually lose my place in the conversation I was having. Be conscious about listening, and you'll be better able to receive feedback.

► **DON'T TAKE NOTES OR RECORD THE CONVERSATION.** This is one not-so-obvious tip that is important for you to understand. It's not just so that you can pay full attention to the person speaking, but if you were to enter a conversation with a notepad or recording device in hand, you're going to change how that person responds. A lot of people get timid in the face of a recording device, and you may end up getting answers you want to hear, rather than those you need to hear.

► **LET THE PERSON SPEAK.** Yes, it's another obvious tip, however sometimes we don't even realize how much we interrupt and stop other people from talking. It's imperative that you let the other person talk after you share your idea. The best information always comes at the end of a person's thought, so give them the floor and let them get to the heart of what they're trying to say. Then guide them even further.

► **DIG DEEPER BY ASKING QUICK FOLLOW-UP QUESTIONS.** Golden information comes the deeper into a conversation you go. As you hear the other person coming to the end of their response, see if you can use some of the quick follow-up questions listed below to have them continue with their thoughts.

  ► *Why do you say that?*

  ► *What else do you think is missing?*

  ► *Why is that important to you?*

➤ *What would be ideal with that?*

➤ *What else comes to mind about that?*

➤ **DON'T JUST LISTEN TO THE WORDS.** In 1971, there was a research study that determined the percentages by which people communicated in different ways. It was through this that the 7-38-55 rule of communication was born. That is, 55% of communication is delivered by body language, 38% from vocal signals, and only 7% is delivered by actual words. I'm not too sure about the exact breakdown—93% of communication from non-verbal signals sounds high—but the reality is that people say a lot using more than their words. Because of this, you need to also pay attention to a person's body language and intonation in addition to their verbal reply. For example, when I was speaking to people about my food truck business, whenever I asked about someone's own personal idea for a food truck, their voices grew louder, they became more animated, and many people would smile big and look toward the sky as they thought about their future restaurant on wheels. This was a key indicator that starting a food truck was something exciting, and helped me validate my ideas even further.

Because you're not actively recording these interactions while they are happening, it's important to record any important discoveries immediately after these conversations happen. Using a notepad that you have handy, or even a portable recording device (like your mobile phone), just make sure to take note of anything that comes to mind that seemed to be important.

You've now made it to the end of the Development Lab—congratulations! You've just put your idea through a series of exercises to turn it into something tangible, and you've even talked about it with others, too! Well done!

By this point, you'll want to go back to your mind map and add anything new that you potentially discovered in your conversations. You may find that your idea has taken a completely different shape altogether. Like in my food truck resource example, you may want to go back out into the wild and share your newly refined idea once again to collect even more information and hone in even more on exactly what you're going to do.

With that said, one final word of caution: positive feedback is not 100% true validation that you've got a winning business on your hands. Just because someone says they like something, and even if their body language further illustrates this, it doesn't mean your target end-user will actually follow through—whether that's subscribing to a website and becoming a fan, or actually purchasing something from you. In Part 4, we'll be putting your refined idea to the test by actually having your target audience validate with their actions, not just with their words. And in some cases, depending on the type of business you have, you may even get paid for the idea that you have in your mind, even before it's built or fully functional.

But before we get there, there's one more series of examinations we need to perform, and it's not about our target idea—it's about our target audience. In Part 3, we'll be going into some heavy (but fun) research to find out exactly who our ideal end-user is, where they congregate, and where they choose to engage. By the end of it you'll have a better understanding of whom you'll be talking to, sometimes better than they do.

Take a moment to breathe. When you're ready, let's get into Part 3 and run research and analysis on exactly the type of person we are trying to reach.

PART 3

FLIGHT PLANNING

" If you can define the problem better than your target customer, they will automatically assume you have the solution."

—JAY ABRAHAM

10

DIAGNOSTICS

B efore a plane can start down the runway, there are a series of evaluations and diagnostic checks that have to occur before it can be cleared for takeoff. There are numerous mechanical and engine checks, of course, but there's another element of the preflight ritual that has to be prepared and analyzed ahead of time too: the overall flight plan.

Besides knowing where to go, pilots have to determine the best way to get there safely, comfortably, and on time. It requires accurate weather forecasts, compliance with air traffic control requirements, and an understanding of how the flight will fit into the existing web of planes that are in the air at the same time. Plus, knowing this information ahead of time can save a ton of money in overall fuel costs.

Pilots have a lot of things working in their favor to help them out. There are several instruments and radars that help a pilot determine the best course to take, and they also rely on others who have recently flown the same route to avoid obstacles like storms and pockets of turbulence.

As the pilot for your own upcoming launch, you've already performed several pre-flight diagnostic checks required for a successful takeoff. In Part 1: Mission Design, you learned more about your strengths and weaknesses, your likes and dislikes, your overall goals and how your target idea fits into that mission. From there, you moved into the Development Lab in Part 2, where your seed idea came alive and grew into something more defined and refined.

Here in Part 3, you're going to explore and assess what the environment in which you are about to fly looks like. Through several guided research exercises, you'll learn everything you need to know about your target audience and where to find them. You'll also discover who else is in the same airspace as you (i.e. what other people and products are serving the same target audience) so you can determine your potential partners, people you should be developing relationships with, and how you can best position yourself and your refined idea amongst the crowd for an effective launch.

Before we get to the research, I need to share an important lesson that I learned quite early in my experience as an entrepreneur. It was a big mindset shift for me that helped me understand what it really takes to build a successful, long-term business in today's connected world. Someone else taught it to me when I started, and I'm happy to pass it along to you now. Flip the page, and here we go…

11

YOUR 1,000 TRUE FANS

t was 3:00 a.m. on February 26th, 2013 and my eyes were still wide open. I couldn't sleep. It felt like when I was a kid about to go to Disneyland the next morning. There were so many thoughts racing through my head, but it wasn't Mickey Mouse or Dole Whip at the Tiki Bar in Adventureland keeping me awake. I was hours away from being interviewed by Andrew Warner on one of my all-time favorite business podcasts: Mixergy.

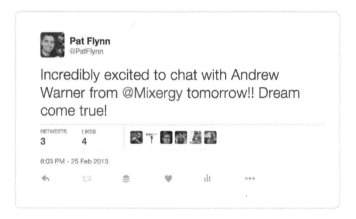

This opportunity had been a long time coming, too. I had been listening to Andrew's podcast for years, and we were supposed to conduct the interview in September, but my daughter's due date was around that time, so we had to delay it. Now, finally, the day had arrived.

What I love about Andrew and his show is that he is a fierce interviewer. He holds nothing back and asks tough questions that no one else dares to ask. I've watched him verbally pin his guests into a corner. It's often cringe-worthy, but so good at the same time.

So why was I excited to step into the ring with Andrew Warner? Well, I have mad respect for him and the quality of his work. As a podcaster myself, I could appreciate all he puts into producing his show, and it was an honor to receive his invitation. The first thing I thought about after I learned I was going to appear on Mixergy was simply how cool it was going to be to speak directly with one of my favorites. As soon as the interview started, however, my nerves kicked in.

I knew he was going to ask tough questions right from the start, which is exactly what he did. The initial conversation was about his reluctance to even have me on the show in the first place. Not quite the introduction I had imagined in my head, but still it was the classic Andrew style, and here I was on the other end. Further into the conversation, after sharing my success with my LEED exam website and how I share that business as an example on my blog and report my numbers month to month publicly, he followed with:

"
Are we thinking too small when we think about examples like that? Like, shouldn't we be thinking, 'What is changing our world today?...How do I create the software, the new spreadsheet of the world?' Because, look at how spreadsheets have touched everybody's lives, and they've improved everything

from students to businesses to just people who are taking notes. Shouldn't we be thinking along those lines instead of, how do I just make more money month-to-month?"

LINK TO INTERVIEW AND TRANSCRIPT FOUND HERE:
HTTP://MIXERGY.COM/INTERVIEWS/PATRICK-FLY-NN-SMART-PASSIVE-INCOME-INTERVIEW/

It was a great question. Was I thinking too small? Was I doing everyone in my audience a disservice by sharing examples of earnings from a business in the architecture industry that most of the world hasn't even heard of?

Here was my reply:

"*Well, really, it's not about the money, it's about helping individual people. Like you said, it's great to think worldly and big and create the next "spreadsheet," but what I think you can do is niche down and change a smaller group of people's world. Right? Taking a specific market and changing their world. Not necessarily creating a spreadsheet for everybody, but maybe a spreadsheet just for people who have 3-year-old kids who are potty training. That will change people's worlds and it will change the person who is sharing that information as well.*"

I could have used a better example, but my wife and I were actually in the middle of potty training our son so I think that's the example that came to mind. Besides that, I was really happy Andrew asked me such a tough question because it allowed me to truly convey the essence of what I teach. That it's not about creating the next spreadsheet, or Facebook or Uber. You can do that and I fully support those who want it, but what I try to teach is that **you don't have to go big in the world to experience success. You just have to be big in somebody's world.**

There's an expression that says, "If you want to make a million dollars, change a million lives." I understand the nature of this expression and appreciate that it's about changing lives, but it's terrible advice. When you're starting a business this can be a completely debilitating thought. In the beginning, it can be tough for anyone to know you exist, let alone a million people, and when you break down the math you should never value yourself and what you have to offer at just $1 per person you serve.

Let's look at the math in a different way.

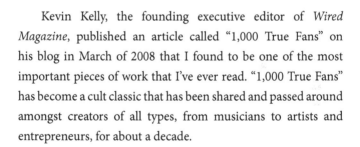

Kevin Kelly, the founding executive editor of *Wired Magazine,* published an article called "1,000 True Fans" on his blog in March of 2008 that I found to be one of the most important pieces of work that I've ever read. "1,000 True Fans" has become a cult classic that has been shared and passed around amongst creators of all types, from musicians to artists and entrepreneurs, for about a decade.

LINK TO "1,000 TRUE FANS":
HTTP://KK.ORG/THETECHNIUM/1000-TRUE-FANS/

The article is extremely powerful because it puts into perspective that success doesn't have to come from a blockbuster hit or chance viral product. It can come by focusing on obtaining only 1,000 true fans.

A true fan, Kevin writes, "is defined as someone who will purchase anything and everything you produce." If you're a musician, they'll drive hundreds of miles to watch your next gig. They read every post, watch every video, and listen to every word of your podcast because it's a part of their daily ritual. They are the ones who have truly fallen in love with what you have to offer the world and will always be there to support you.

And here's where math plays a role, according to Kevin:

"

Assume conservatively that your True Fans will each spend one day's wages per year in support of what you do. That 'one-day-wage' is an average, because of course your truest fans will spend a lot more than that. Let's peg that per diem each True Fan spends at $100 per year. If you have 1,000 fans that sums up to $100,000 per year, which minus some modest expenses, is a living for most folks.

One thousand is a feasible number. You could count to 1,000. If you added one fan a day, it would take only three years. True Fanship is doable. Pleasing a True Fan is pleasurable, and invigorating. It rewards the artist to remain true, to focus on the unique aspects of their work, the qualities that True Fans appreciate."

To sum up the math, if you had only 1,000 true fans who each paid you $100 a year, you would be making $100,000 per year. A lot of people pay more than $100 per month for services they hardly use, so a person willing to spend $100 a year for something they truly love isn't all that hard to grasp.

Don't worry too much about the specific numbers being used here, and if you're not the type of person who enjoys being front and center in your brand, don't worry—you don't have to.

The main idea is that in this world of seven billion people, there are a lot of sub-worlds to which you can become or create a trusted resource, product, or service that those people need or want. You don't need those sub-worlds to be huge in order to make a difference in the lives of others, and your own.

So to go back to Andrew's question. Was I thinking too small? No, I wasn't. I was thinking small enough.

THE RICHES ARE IN THE NICHES

I heard this phrase once that has stuck with me ever since I started doing business online. It didn't come from Kevin's article specifically, but it beautifully sums up his point:

The Riches are in the Niches

As you conduct your market research, you'll begin to uncover these sub-worlds within this world that you're targeting, markets whose people begin to have similarities in their problems, behaviors, habits and needs and wants and desires. You are allowed to, and I encourage you, to narrow down who your target audience is because as you'll learn in this upcoming section, the more you can narrow down your niche, the better you can serve them, the easier they will connect with you, and the less competition you'll have along the way.

Remember, only a handful of people even know what the LEED exam is, but when people were looking for help to study for that exam, I became their trusted resource. They were happy to buy from me and recommend me to others.

To get you started in the research of your target audience and the market that you'll be serving, we're going to uncover what's going on in the space already so you can determine how to add a new flavor to what is already being served.

12

THE MARKET MAP

Have you ever heard the expression "stand out from the crowd?"

It's an idiom that's used to describe something that is unusual or unlike the other things around it. It's also a piece of advice that is almost as overused and undefined as "think outside the box" and "take it to the next level."

In order to benefit from any of these phrases, the noun must first be defined. We need to know what kind of box we're in before that we can think outside of it. What level are we at now, what does the next one look like, and at what point do these levels actually change? From what *crowd* are we standing out?

In this chapter, you're going to define the box, level, or crowd—the places, people and products that already serve your target audience. This is what I like to call a market map. With this market map, you'll get a bird's-eye perspective of the environment to which you are about to enter. You will be able to find your place and navigate through it with confidence. Down the road, this map will become an extremely useful guide that you'll likely reference time and time again as you launch, grow, and monetize your business.

Before we begin our research, I must warn you that you'll likely to find other businesses or products that are similar to the one you're developing. Don't let that stop you. In the thousands of conversations and the surveys I've conducted with future entrepreneurs, the number two reason why people hesitate to get started is because they've found out that someone else has already taken their idea. The number one reason is the fear of failure.

If you find that others have already done what you're planning to do, that's a great thing! Someone else has already done the heavy lifting for you. They've taken the time and have spent the money to serve that audience, or attempt to do so, and by following their lead you can determine what's working and what's not, and adjust your business accordingly. You then find your own unique position in that space—something different. That's how you stand out. Keep that in mind as you conduct your research, because as author and speaker Sally Hogshead once said:

" *Different is better than better.*"

Let's get started.

CREATE YOUR MARKET MAP

To create your market map, we're going to find the 3-P's within your market:

► Places
► People
► Products

Each of these items should be organized into their own separate spreadsheet, each with three columns: *name, web address, notes.*

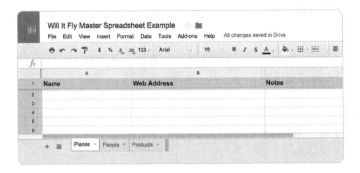

TIP: *I recommend creating one master file to house each of these three separate sheets, plus a few others that we'll be creating in later sections of this book. Both Microsoft Excel and Numbers for Mac allow you to create these sub-sheets within a single file, however I recommend using Google Drive to create a single Google Sheet that can be easily accessible on any device. Places, People and Products will each become a sub-sheet for the exercises you'll be conducting in this section.*

In Chapter 12: The Market Map in the Will It Fly? *Companion Course, I included a video walking you through the process of exactly how to set up a free Google Sheet for this section.*

PLACES

No matter what kind of business you're looking to build, even if it's an offline brick and mortar store, you need to find out where your target audience resides online. During the research phase, this allows you to not only know what other websites exist in the space, but it helps you learn more about who they are. Through comments and forums, you'll be able to hear directly from the voice of your end-user and use that information to help shape what you create, and how you share it.

The results of this exercise will become a list of places where you could potentially advertise or submit articles to gain exposure and build authority and trust in the market.

There are a number of tools available that can help us quickly find the top websites that serve our market, but no other tool is quicker and smarter than Google. So let's start there.

BLOGS

First, we're going to quickly find the top blogs in your niche. We're specifically looking for blogs because they can provide us with three great advantages at this stage:

1. Blogs will often have communities where one can interact with an end-user.

2. It's typically much easier to find or reach the owner of the site.

3. If up-to-date, it can give us a good beat on what's hot and trending.

Fortunately, there's an easy way to filter your search results and spare you the time of sifting through general sites. To find blogs related to your topic, type in the following into a blank Google search field:

BLOG: KEYWORD

Keyword, of course, should be replaced with a word or phrase related to your business or target audience. So for example, if you were going to create a product in the fly fishing industry, you would type:

BLOG: FLY FISHING

Looking at the first page only, you can already begin to see a number of potentially helpful results to include on our list.

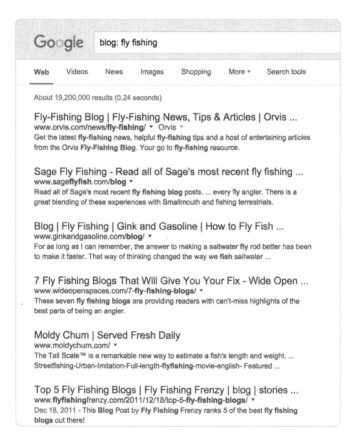

Sometimes, you'll come across a type of article called a list post, which is a collection of helpful resources all in one place. They can be very useful in your hunt for popular websites too:

7 Fly Fishing Blogs That Will Give You Your Fix - Wide Open ...
www.wideopenspaces.com/7-fly-fishing-blogs/ ▾
These seven fly fishing blogs are providing readers with can't-miss highlights of the best parts of being an angler.

Moldy Chum | Served Fresh Daily
www.moldychum.com/ ▾
The Tail Scale™ is a remarkable new way to estimate a fish's length and weight. ...
Streetfishing-Urban-Imitation-Full-length-flyfishing-movie-english- Featured ...

Top 5 Fly Fishing Blogs | Fly Fishing Frenzy | blog | stories ...
www.flyfishingfrenzy.com/2011/12/18/top-5-fly-fishing-blogs/ ▾
Dec 18, 2011 - This Blog Post by Fly Fishing Frenzy ranks 5 of the best fly fishing blogs out there!

Another helpful tip is to click on the links in the "Searches related to" section located at the bottom of the results page. These are other popular terms that relate to your search. It'll show you what else people are seeking out.

Searches related to best fly fishing blog

fly fishing **blogspot**	**saltwater** fly fishing blog
fly fishing blog **sites**	**orvis** fly fishing blog
delta trout force	**chuck kashner** fly fishing blog
learning to fly fish trout	fly fishing **forum**

Gooooooooogle ›

1 2 3 4 5 6 7 8 9 10   Next

After clicking on "fly fishing blog sites" in this area, the results page for that search term found a few of the same sites as before, but one new one in the fifth position that was golden:

Top 5 Fly Fishing Blogs | Fly Fishing Frenzy | blog | stories ...
www.**flyfishing**frenzy.com/2011/12/18/**top-5-fly-fishing-blogs**/ ▾
Dec 18, 2011 - This **Blog** Post by **Fly Fishing** Frenzy ranks 5 of the best **fly fishing blogs** out there!

Sage Fly Fishing Blog
www.sageflyfish.com/**blog** ▾
Read all of Sage's most recent **fly fishing blog** posts.

The 5 Best Fly Tying Blogs You Should be Following
duranglers.com/5-best-**fly-tying-blogs**-following/ ▾
Oct 22, 2014 - Until then, here are (in our opinion) the 5 Best Fly Tying **Blogs** you need to be following right now: ... The Easy E Hopper by the Hopper **Fishing Blog** ... I hope these **sites** can help kickstart your fall and winter **fly** tying. Keep an ...

Blog | Fly Fishing | Gink and Gasoline | How to Fly Fish ...
www.ginkandgasoline.com/**blog**/ ▾
It's time to share your best **fly fishing** photos from 2015 and win some great gear! ... One of the great things about having a website and **blog** is the interaction I ...

50 Best Fishing Blogs - Zen College Life
www.zencollegelife.com/50-best-**fishing-blogs**/ ▾
Switters B – Nicely written **blog** about improving your **fly fishing** skills ... Hunting & Fishing – Interesting read with some great tips and giveaways from other **sites**.

Score! Already we've found over 70 different blogs that talk about fly fishing—and that was only with one single seed keyword! That may seem overwhelming, but we'll be conducting more research on these later. Think of what we're doing as panning for gold. We're putting a load of gravel and sand into our pan, and through carefully calculated movements, we'll eventually see the stuff that matters.

Not all niches lend themselves very well to blogging, however, so if you're having trouble locating blogs in your space try other seed keywords that relate to your target audience and market first. If nothing comes up, move onto the next exercise. There are several other types of locations your audience may be living online.

Be sure to fill in your spreadsheet as you go along, and make those bad boys clickable for easy clicking later on. Include any special notes in the Notes section of your spreadsheet too—anything from those resources that seem to stand out to you. After that's complete, let's find out what the end-users have to say. It's time to find some forums.

FORUMS

Forums, like blogs, are a fantastic resource for anyone doing research in any given niche. Unlike blogs, however, which are typically authored by one person or a small team, forums are collections of end-user generated conversations (also known as threads). The forum owners are harder to find, but in terms of research, this is like panning for gold during the California gold rush.

To find forums in your niche, it's the same deal as with blogs. Type in the following into a blank Google search field:

FORUM: FLY FISHING

And again, we've got some positive results:

Try other keywords and use the "searches related to" links at the bottom of your searches to get as many "first page" forum results as possible in your spreadsheet. There are typically fewer forums than there are blogs because they are more difficult to manage (and because the top ones simply overpower the rest), so try to add five to 10 of the top forums to your Places column.

I'll show you how to pan for gold here later. For now, let's keep going. There are a few more locations we need to check before we move onto the next part of your market map.

SOCIAL MEDIA GROUPS

Almost the entire world lives on social media, which means our target audience is likely there, too. And typically, they've found others just like them. Seeking out your end-users on social media can help you find real-time conversations about anything and everything related to your niche, which can be a powerful tool for you as you begin to build your business and research your target audience.

There are several social media channels online, however the ones that are most convenient to potentially find groups of your end-users are on Facebook and LinkedIn.

Now, depending on your niche, one will likely be more useful than the other. For example, if you're looking for a skateboarding group it's going to be less likely that you'll find one on the professional social network, LinkedIn, although you might be surprised. On the other hand, Facebook is typically more universal, ranging in topics from DIY Crafts to DIY Brain Surgery (not kidding).

To search on Facebook, simply go to the top of your Facebook page and type in a keyword related to your niche in the search bar and hit enter. From there, you'll get a nice results page with a number of different sections. What you want to look for is the "groups" section, which may be hidden under the "more" tab, as seen on the next page:

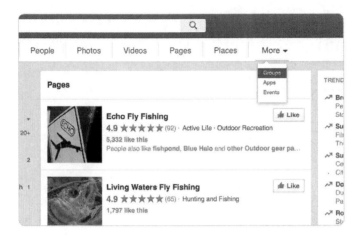

After clicking through you'll get a huge list of groups where people who are interested in that particular topic are centrally located. There will be dozens, potentially hundreds or even thousands of groups, depending on the niche. Some are public and can be joined immediately without any request for approval, while others will require you to wait for the administrator to approve your membership. Choose the ones that are the most populated and make sure they're active before you list them in your spreadsheet. You can do that by clicking into the group (again, it must be a public group in order for you to get immediate access) and seeing when the last messages were shared. If it was last year, then it's not an active community worth including. If there were conversations from the recent past, then take note, and find the next active group.

You can find targeted groups in LinkedIn, as well. For both sites, however, please note that you have to be logged in to get access to the groups.

See if you can come up with at least 25 notable groups

across both channels, if applicable. At this point, along with the blogs and forums you've collected, you're likely to have over 100 different entries on your Places sheet. If you have more, that's great! If you have less, that's fine, too. In all likelihood, no matter how many you have listed, you've done a lot more research than most people who are already serving your target niche. You should feel good about yourself and already have a nice impression of what's out there.

We're not done yet though, because now we're going to seek out the top people and influencers in the space, using completely different Ninja Gaiden tactics.

PEOPLE

It's not just important to understand where your target audience is, but it's also beneficial for you to learn who is in the space already serving them, too. By identifying existing authorities that your target audience already trusts, you can collect massive insight as to how your audience behaves, what they respond to, and what they ignore. In other words, you can see what works and what doesn't.

You'll be able to follow these top players in the space, learn how they interact and engage with their audience (and each other), and begin to determine precisely who you should foster a relationship with down the road, and figure out what you can do to separate yourself from the collective whole.

When I began following the top players in the Internet marketing space, for example, I subscribed to as many newsletters as I could. There were about 30 of them and every day I would receive multiple emails from this assembly of influencers. After a few weeks I had hundreds of emails and I began to notice some interesting and useful patterns.

For one, I could see that each of them was extremely well versed when it came to copywriting. They paid careful attention to the words they chose to use to describe the products they were offering to me. Additionally, I started to pinpoint groups within the top tier of influencers in the space who would often send emails out at the same time about the same product or promotion. I started to notice who was friends with whom, and eventually I discovered the inner circles simply by paying attention. This taught me the importance of building key relationships and how JV (joint venture) partnerships worked within the space.

All of that was very useful to me, but the most useful education I learned from following the top influencers in the space was what NOT to do. I saw what everyone else was doing, and I purposefully brought something different to the space.

I learned, for example, that almost every email sent out by these influencers did not include my name in it. They all started with "Hey friend" or just went right into the content of the email. And the content within those emails were mainly pitches for products and services, and there was little to no value given before the pitch. There was no attempt to interact with me or learn more about my needs and wants. Consequently, when I built my own email list, I made a clear effort to separate myself from this group. I always make sure to collect people's names so that I can address each person by their first name, and I consciously made the decision to not sell directly on my email list. I wouldn't recommend that for everyone, but the "do the opposite of everyone else" strategy is a powerful one. I still continue to get emails from people today letting me know how much of a breath of fresh air my emails are in the space of Internet marketing and entrepreneurship.

That's what you want to be—a breath of fresh air to your audience. As you move forward into this next exercise, try to think about how you can be a breath of fresh air. What do you need to bring to the lot in order to give oxygen and life back to your audience, which may be tired of the same old stuff or looking for that missing puzzle piece?

Let's begin to construct a list of influencers in our space. As you discover who they are, write down their name, website address, and add any special notes in the People sheet in your master spreadsheet. You may know a number of influencers in your space already, and if so, add them to the list. To help you find more, here are three different methods for locating them.

TOP SOCIAL MEDIA PROFILES

Quite appropriately, social media platforms become an easy target for us to dig deep into to discover who the influencers are within a given space. Not only that, with influencers usually come followers, and so there's a lot we can eventually learn about the market in which you're about to position yourself. Let's start with Twitter.

Twitter is a fantastic resource, not just for seeing what your favorite celebrities are up to, but also for finding top influencers in your niche. The number of followers a person or profile has is a relatively decent indication of their authority in a space, because people typically choose to follow accounts they find interesting and useful. It's not a perfect barometer, however, because some of the numbers could be skewed as many accounts go inactive, and some people even go as far as to purchase followers in order to increase their perceived authority, which is lame. In general, however, the number followers a person has is a good indication of their standing within their niche.

Beyond that, Twitter is the social media channel I'd recommended above all others to start with when you begin building your brand because it's relatively much faster to build a following on than any other platform. It's also a great medium for starting relationships with influencers. Whether you already have a Twitter account or not, you can still continue forward with this part of your research.

To find the top Twitter profiles in your niche, we're going to start on Twitter's advanced search function, which you can find at **HTTPS://TWITTER.COM/SEARCH-ADVANCED.**

On this page, you'll notice a number of different fields to hone in on any kind of search you wish. You're welcome to play around with this and narrow down your search results, but the only text fields we'll be worrying about to start are the "All of these words" field, and the "From this date" field.

In the "all of these words" text field, simply type in the primary keyword that you've been using for your other searches related to your niche. You can run as many searches as you'd like with other keywords later.

In the "from this date" text field, select a date range that spans the previous two months only. This ensures that any accounts we come up with are active.

The results page can be a little overwhelming, but also extremely interesting, especially with the images you might find on the page. Before you get sucked into a wormhole and lose your place, click on the "More options" tab at the top, and select "Top Accounts."

This will give you a list of the top accounts that have been sharing updates (tweeting) about that particular topic. Twitter has built an algorithm to rank these results in your favor, likely taking into account not just the number of followers, but other things like how active their followers are, too.

Before you begin to save these profiles in your spreadsheet (collecting both the name of the account or person and the web address to their website, if they have one. If not, simply add a link to their Twitter profile), click through to each of the profiles to make sure they align with your target audience. Although Twitter's search algorithm is advanced, it's not always perfect. Just make sure the profiles and their recent updates look legitimate, and then enter those accounts into your database. I'd shoot for collecting at least 20 from Twitter, but if there are more that seem to be influencer material, by all means, add those to your database, too.

In the fly fishing niche, for example, we can see that the top ranking Twitter profile is called Orvis News, with the username @OrvisFlyFishing. Clicking through, we see they have 36.7k followers—yep, this is exactly the type of profile to include on our spreadsheet.

With that said, not all influential profiles have to have tens of thousands of followers. Accounts with a small number of followers can still be incredibly useful. Twitter ranks accounts by the amount of activity happening on the page, not just on the size of one's following. If an account with relatively fewer followers shows up within the top few rows of your search results page and looks legitimate, enter it into your spreadsheet. These "smaller" accounts could actually prove to be more useful for you. It will likely be easier to reach out and build a relationship with the person behind the handle.

OTHER SOCIAL MEDIA PLATFORMS

There are a number of other social media platforms where you can search for influencers. I'm not going to spend time going through the details of how to search through each of them, but they follow a similar path to what we did on Twitter. Some of these social media channels are better for certain niches than others, so I recommend you explore around and collect names of influencers within each of these platforms who seem to have collected a large, active following:

- Facebook
- Instagram
- LinkedIn
- Periscope

Beyond social media, there are two more giant search engines that you can use to find influencers. The first one is obvious, and that's YouTube. YouTube is, for some influencers, their primary medium for building a business and connecting with their audience, so search around using various keywords related to your niche and find those with large numbers of subscribers, and make sure to add them onto your spreadsheet.

The other much less obvious search engine happens to be my favorite: iTunes.

✒

ITUNES

When we think of iTunes we don't normally think of it as a search engine, but that's in fact what it is. It's a directory of music, videos, books, apps and podcasts that have not only revolutionized how people consume and manage their media, but it has also become a way to understand where (and to whom) we should be paying attention.

In particular, podcasts have been incredible for on-the-go entertainment and education, and because anyone can create a podcast and there's no barrier to entry in terms of who can and cannot publish a show, we get a transparent look at who has influence in the space we're researching. Furthermore, certain podcasts have huge audiences that cannot be found in other forms of media on the web; so finishing off our gold panning expedition in the iTunes river can yield some extremely unique nuggets of information.

There are two ways that we can search through iTunes to determine who may have some influence:

1. Looking at the top ranked and rated podcasts related to your niche.

2. Finding who has been interviewed on shows related to your niche.

To get a quick understanding of the top podcasts in iTunes, open up the iTunes Application on your computer. You could use your mobile device to conduct this same research, however using the desktop platform opens up other functionality that will come in handy during this research.

TIP: *If you don't have access to iTunes, you could also search through the Stitcher app on your mobile device. Stitcher is another top podcasting directory with search functionality only available on mobile, for more or less similar results.*

In the search field within iTunes, type in your target keyword and hit enter. Under "Podcasts" (not "Podcast Episodes"), click on "See All":

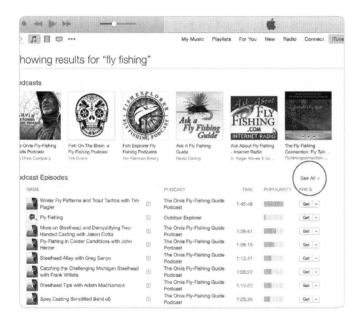

This will give you a huge matrix of podcasts people have created related to your niche. Like with Twitter and other social media platforms, iTunes' search functionality comes with its own secret algorithm, but in general the ones with the most authority are at the top:

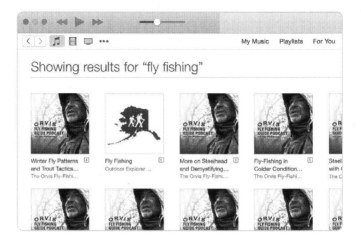

Once again, the Orvis fly fishing brand shows up in our results. They seem to be everywhere! This tells us that this is a prominent brand that has a lot of authority in the space, and it's definitely one to pay attention to. If you see brands like this pop up during your research, give them a **bold** indication, which will help remind you that these are some the top players in the niche.

Let's click through to *The Orvis Fly Fishing Guide Podcast* and see what we come up with:

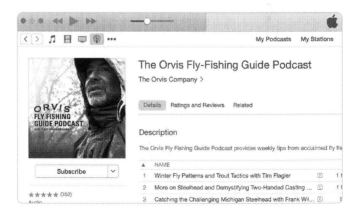

On this page, we can gather a lot of information. The host of the show is Tom Rosenbauer. Good to know if we were going to reach out for an introduction. Second, under "Links" on the left-hand side, we have a convenient link to their website.

Above that, we see the overall rating for the show: 345 reviews at a 5-star rating. The audience loves it! And so do we because this means it's a great show and we should dig deeper. If you come across a 1- to 3-star show, move onto the next one. It's not worth your focus at this time.

Take note of the name of each podcast and its host within your spreadsheet. Be sure to also take note of who else might have been featured on this particular show. Not all, but several of the episodes in *The Orvis Fly Fishing Guide Podcast* feature a guest.

There's Greg Senyo who talks about Steelhead, John Herzer who talks about fly fishing in colder conditions, and Kip Veith, who shares tips about fishing for smallmouth bass. Although these people don't necessarily have a ton of influence, they can be important people to note for future reference. Put their name on your spreadsheet and jot down their expertise. Those can also come in handy later.

That last iTunes podcast tip I have for you is to make sure you visit the "Related" section, typically located in its own tab or button underneath the main title of the podcast. These are the other shows subscribed to by listeners of the podcast. This can give you a great crumb trail to other top influential podcasters in the space. I recommend you run similar research as we did above with those podcasts, too.

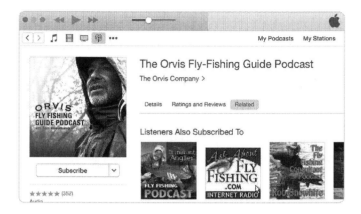

BUZZSUMO

BuzzSumo (**BUZZSUMO.COM**) is probably the best search tool available on the market to help you find influencers and the content they are promoting. So why wait until now to mention it? Because it's not free to use.

I wanted to show you that you don't need to pay for anything to complete your research. All too often, brand new entrepreneurs come out of the gate buying every product and tool, left and right, only to be left with a bunch of software and courses that never get put to use. I don't want you to be one of those "toolpreneurs." By going the free, manual route you're not only able to save some dough, but more importantly you understand the process that a lot of these tools can automate for you. If you simply just dive into the tool then what have you learned beyond just how to use that tool? Not much.

Don't get me wrong though, I LOVE automation and having tools and team members to help me automate the processes in my business, and I recommend that as you grow your business you look for how to do the same. But at this point, you're very much in the trenches, and that allows you to have the field of vision you need to properly navigate your space.

Now, if you do want to invest money each month into a tool to help you with more insights in and around your target market, BuzzSumo is the way to go. I won't get into the details of how to use the tool here, but it's fairly easy to understand and the guided tour explains along the way if you're interested.

By now, you should have a healthy amount of important people who play some influential role in this market, be it authorities in the space or experts. Fifty is a good number to shoot for, but more or less, you've already found who you need to find for now. To finish off our market map, we're going to explore the realm of products to discover what's being offered, and what people in your niche are willing to buy.

PRODUCTS

This is likely one of the most useful areas of research within your niche. You're going to find the top products, services, and books that are being offered to your audience. In other words, what are they willing to pay for right now?

By looking at what your audience is buying, you'll be able to determine what kinds of offerings already exist, and what else might be missing. We've done some of that already, but this is especially important because we are looking at what's being sold and purchased—not just websites that people can visit for free (though those are, of course, important). When people lay down their money for a product or service, they are either getting what they really need and/or are being sold to in a way that really works. Both of these are good to know.

Now, before we continue, please note that there's a difference between what is being offered, and what is being purchased. Just because there's an offer on a website it doesn't necessarily mean anyone is buying it, even if the site says that's the case. It's still important to see what's out there even if it's not selling, and we'll get to that, but first let's visit a site where there are hundreds of millions of buyers and a ton of data to show us exactly what they are purchasing and their feedback: **AMAZON.COM**.

AMAZON.COM

AMAZON.COM, for all intensive purposes, is a search engine. Like all of the other search engines we've already used in this section, you can type in a keyword and you'll get the top results. But unlike the others, people come to Amazon to look for things to buy, and that makes it all the more powerful.

Type in your target keyword or niche into the search bar in Amazon and take note of what pops up. The results are ranked based on popularity (and again, what people are buying), so no matter if it's a book, gadget, or any other physical product, write it down and include its link in your spreadsheet. We'll come back to these later for something even more revealing, but for now, just start compiling a list of products—their names, a web address to the product, and at the same time take note of the average rating, the number of reviews, and the current price point. Add these to the Products tab in your master spreadsheet.

For example, this Wild Water Fly Fishing Complete $^5/_6$ Starter Package, as shown, has 144 customer reviews with a 4.5 average rating, and it sells for $94.00.

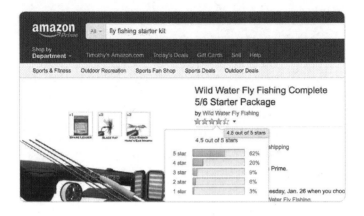

If you were only able to find physical products, add a few books into your list, too. Select "books" from the dropdown menu next to the search bar and hit enter. You'll come up with a list of books related to your niche that you should enter into your spreadsheet.

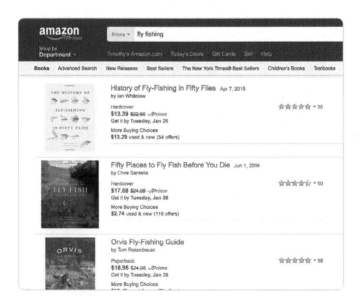

And there are those Orvis guys again, sitting in spot #3. They've got this niche covered! And remember, that's a good thing for you.

Before we move onto other places on the web to find products to add to your list, because we're here, there's one more part of **AMAZON.COM** I'd like to mention that will enable you to quickly and easily add a list of a dozen or more influencers into your People list.

On the left hand side of the book search results page, there's a section titled "Author," with a list of the top authors who have written books about that particular niche. Write these names down, because not only do they potentially have influence, but they would also be great to potentially reach out to for collaboration.

Next, we're going to have to dig a little deeper to find some other existing products that are offered in your space, and we are going to start with another section of your list that you've already filled out: your Places.

This list is important because communication is happening in your audience right now, and a lot of those conversations are often about what programs and items people are interested in buying, or have tried and reviewed. Yes, you could go to Google for information about more products, but it's much easier to trust people who are having actual conversations about products. You can gauge the reaction and excitement (or lack thereof) for a particular product or offering.

Start by picking your top forum and look for the area where there are various boards and discussion threads. Find the search bar or a search function. These won't exist in all forums, but many do include a search function. If not, you'll have to manually scan the discussions, which is okay because people like to start discussions about various products serving that space, and if they are there they should be easy to find. In the search bar, look for inquiries like:

- "Product review"
- "Have you tried"
- "I bought"
- "I purchased"

These terms will almost always point you to discussion threads where conversations about existing products already exist. If you find them, copy and paste the discussion link into your spreadsheet, as well as the link to the product itself if it isn't already listed in your spreadsheet.

At this point, you will have collected a number of various products, books and services that people in your space are using. If you still have room for more, here's what you can do to fill in the rest:

Type in keywords related to your niche in Google. In the sidebar, you'll see a number of products and services that are paying to be shown there through Google's advertising network. Write these down. Now, although we can't be sure if these are selling, we at least know there's a company out there promoting this product with a little bit of money and marketing behind it.

You could also type in "product review" alongside your keyword in Google as well, and you'll come across a slew of products and offerings for your target niche. Beware, because a lot of these product review sites are made to look like real reviews, when they are made by people simply to rank high on Google and get in front of search engine traffic.

You can also visit some of the blogs or websites that you collected as well in your first column to see what those people may be offering. There may be links to services or products in the sidebar of those websites, or on a particular page called "resources" or "products"—all of which could be helpful in filling in your list.

Again, you're looking to get a sense of what already exists out there and where you might fit. Don't worry about how you'll fit in quite yet; although after your research you may find that it is very easy to see what's missing and what you could do to add value to this existing community. Other times, it's not so obvious and you'll need to dig a little deeper, which is what we will all do in the next section. We're going to make specific conclusions about our target audience and our prospective end-user.

PAT FLYNN

13

THE CUSTOMER
P.L.A.N.

Over the last several pages, your radar has been programmed to measure the climate of the market on which you have set your sights. You discovered exactly where your target audience resides, who the top influencers are, and even what products are being offered in the space.

I'd like to reiterate, once again, that you're doing an amazing job. Not everyone who is building a business is doing as much research as you are (and that includes those who have already built successful businesses). Those who became successful did so because they took action, and so will you. However what we've been doing is going to drastically shorten the time you need to figure it out after you start.

Your initial idea has likely taken new shape through the exercises we have completed, from the mind mapping to talking about your idea with others, to everything you've just discovered about your target market. You may have even come up with something completely brand new along the way, which is cool. My job is to help you explore different options, both in terms of how your idea will succeed in the market, and also how it fits for you.

With that being said, the ironic part of taking charge and building a business for yourself is that in order for it to succeed, you have to realize that the business is actually not about you at all. It's about serving your target customer.

You've heard me use the word serve several times in this book, and it's because that's exactly what you have to do. Your earnings are a byproduct of how well you serve your audience, and you can only best serve your audience when you know exactly who they are, what they're going through, and what will get them to take action.

In this chapter, we're going to dig deep into understanding your target customer. We've already done a lot of the research on the market, but now we're going to get into the mind and emotion of your end-user so that you know exactly what they're going through, and how we can best provide a solution. Some people call this defining your customer avatar, or making a customer profile. Those are fine descriptions, but I prefer to guide you into something more specific and actionable: your Customer P.L.A.N.

Your Customer P.L.A.N. is broken down into four sections, in this specific order:

1. Problems

2. Language

3. Anecdotes

4. Needs

After you discover your Customer P.L.A.N., you'll know exactly how your target idea fits into your target audience. You can then align and adjust accordingly before we test this out to give yourself the best chance of landing on something they'll buy.

Although we've talked about our target audience, end-user, reader, listener, viewer, and subscriber throughout this book, it's important that we switch our mindset at this point into discovering and describing our target customer. We are, in fact, creating a business, and it's important that we make sure you will be able to generate an income from the service and products that you'll be providing.

When you serve you get paid back in return, but only if you give those you serve a way to pay you back in some way, shape, or form.

Before we get into the Customer P.L.A.N., you might be wondering why we waited so long to finally begin learning about the target customer. Shouldn't that have been done first?

My answer is no. This was not a mistake and careful consideration has been taken to include this section where I felt it would have the most impact. Let me tell you why.

If you were to start a business completely from scratch, with no ideas in mind, then my answer would be the opposite. I would say, yes, you start by seeking out a particular market and honing in on their pains and problems and extract a solution from there. The potential consequence, however, may be that you enter a niche that you're not really interested in, nor care to serve.

But that isn't what's going on here. You aren't starting from scratch. You had an idea in mind before you picked up this book. Or maybe you had a lot of ideas. Most people who express interest in starting a business of their own have not one, but several ideas racing through their brain, and the challenge becomes which one to focus on first. It's a dilemma that keeps a lot of would-be entrepreneurs from starting at all.

I forced you to pick one and then run it through a series

of thought experiments and exercises designed to define and refine your idea. At the same time you were honing in on what kind of business worked for you. As you progressed into market research, every new exercise you completed became further validation that this was a market you were interested in serving.

Will your initial idea match the needs of your target customer? Maybe. We'll find out as we move through this book, but if it doesn't that's okay. What's important is that you know what works for you, and you know this is a market you'd like to serve. Using the Customer P.L.A.N., you'll be able to align the two in a way that gives you confidence and energy moving forward.

So let's not wait any longer. Let's start to map out your Customer P.L.A.N.

PREPARE YOUR MASTER SPREADSHEET

To help you organize the research you're about to do, we're going to add one additional sub-sheet to your master spreadsheet. Title the sheet P.L.A.N, and then add headings to four separate columns: Problems, Language, Anecdotes, and Needs. Then, keep reading.

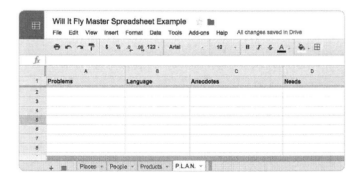

P:

PROBLEMS

A business idea is really just a potential solution to a target customer's pain or problem. The better you can solve that person's problem, the more successful your business will become. So of course, this all starts with finding the pain. When you can extract the pain, the marketing almost takes care of itself.

Unfortunately, too many people just dive into their business without a true understanding of their potential customer. They might have an idea, but they never take the time to get to the core of the pains and problems plaguing the people they're trying to serve.

You're on the right track though, because you're about to learn how you can figure that out.

1-TO-1 REAL TIME CONVERSATIONS

By far, the best way to research anything related to your target customer is to have a real-time, one-on-one conversation with them. Emails are okay, but an in-person or over-the-phone conversation will serve you much better. In Part 2 you had conversations with all kinds of people to help poke holes in your idea it and refine it, but in order to get to the true pain point of your target customer, you need to speak to your target customers, and you need to ask the right questions.

In Episode #46 of my podcast (**SMARTPASSIVEINCOME. COM/SESSION46**), Dane Maxwell from The Foundation spoke about how important asking the right questions are in extracting the true pains that you could potentially solve as an entrepreneur. In that episode, he listed a number of fantastic questions that you could ask anyone to learn more about what they potentially need:

- ► What's something about [topic] that frustrates you?

- ► If you had a magic wand and could change anything related to [topic] what would it be?

- ► What problems are costing you the most money right now?

- ► What's the most important activity related to [topic] that you do? Is there any frustration associated with that?

- ► What related to [topic] takes up the most time?

- ► Do you use anything to help you with [topic] already? What do you like about it? What do you wish was better?

- ► What's something related to [topic] that you have to keep doing over and over again?

Most importantly, when having these conversations, *always* dig deeper. Follow up their replies with, "how come," or, "why do you feel that way," and you'll be able to understand the true drivers behind any frustrations or pains the person may have.

Where do you find your target customers that you could speak to? You have a spreadsheet that already lists the places where these people exist, which is where I would start. You could potentially get to know people on those forums and get to a point where you could ask for a one-on-one conversation with them over the phone, on Skype, or through a direct messaging system on that platform.

The best place I've been able to find people to speak to, however, are offline at conventions and other events where I know those people will exist. In my opinion, there is nothing better than face-to-face interaction.

Keep note of which people you speak to and what their pains and problems are in your spreadsheet. These people could become a great sounding board for various items related to your business, and of course, a future customer. And again, make sure you give them something in return for all the help they're providing you.

SURVEYS

If it seems like a one-on-one conversation isn't going to happen anytime soon, another proven method for learning about the pains and problems of your target customer is to conduct a survey. Surveys are powerful because you can potentially collect a load of data about your target customer (and their pain points) in a relatively short period of time.

By far, the top resource for learning how to conduct a proper business-related survey is a book titled *Ask*, by Ryan Levesque. After reading Ryan's book twice, I ran a survey on my blog in mid-2015 that revealed that I wasn't doing nearly as much as I could to serve my audience in the best way possible. I made massive changes to my overall content strategy based on the results, and it's one of the major reasons why this book even exists today.

If you'd like to hear a condensed version of his book, and its impact on my own business and brand, you can listen to my interview with Ryan Levesque in Episode #178 of my podcast (**SMARTPASSIVEINCOME.COM/SESSION178**)

We'll get into the basics of how to promote your survey in just a minute, but like with the one-on-one conversations you'll be having with your target customer, the most important element of any survey are the questions that you ask.

There is one question in particular, however, that is the most important question you can ask your target customer. You should never ask questions about what people will buy, but you can ask questions like this one that will help them tell you the answer.

What's your #1 biggest challenge related to [topic]?

As you can see, this question is similar to questions we ask in our one-on-one conversations. In Ryan's "Deep Dive" survey (one of four important survey types he shares in the book), this is the very first and most important question you can ask, and if you had the chance to ask only one, this one would be it.

What's nice about this question is that it's simple, but at the same time, amazingly powerful. It's open-ended so it's going to take time to analyze the results, but your answers will almost always come back in a form that is useful for you, with real accounts of your target customer's struggles.

A byproduct of this exercise will be that you can take note of the language that your target customer uses in their reply, which will be useful in the next section of your P.L.A.N. On many occasions, parts of their reply can be directly inserted into future promotional materials for your business, like emails, product descriptions and sales pages.

> Tip: *As you collect responses from your target customer about their pains and problems, add any notable words and phrases into the Language column in your P.L.A.N. spreadsheet.*

If you already have a following related to your target market, send emails to your list or messages to your social media following with this single question. Include context about why it's important and why you're asking, but keep it short and sweet so that you will get more honest replies.

If you don't already have an audience, a following, or an email list, don't fret. You can still conduct an extremely revealing survey with your target customers with no current contacts. I know, because I've been able to do this too.

Back in Part 2, I shared how **FOODTRUCKR.COM** evolved through several conversations I had with all different kinds of people, including local food truck owners here in my own neighborhoods in San Diego. Even before the site went up, I was able to survey hundreds of food truck owners from around the country to determine what their struggles were and what product I could potentially create to help them. How was I able to reach them? By emailing them.

Some had their email address posted on their website, while I had to ask others for an email address through Twitter.

Because I was creating this site for both food truck owners, and those who were just starting out, the single question I came up with was:

What's the ONE thing you wish you'd known before you started your food truck?

After compiling a list of 250 food truck owners' email addresses, I sent emails one-by-one, personalizing them as best as I could based on the name of the truck, location, and anything else interesting I found through my research.

After a week, I received about eight responses. That's not a huge percentage (3.2%), but the responses that did come back were quite eye-opening, especially considering I didn't know much about this industry beyond the fact that garlic-parmesan french fries were my kryptonite. Here are a few responses to that email below:

Response 1

" *I wish I would have known what all went into the permitting process and how involved it is so that I could have been more prepared and ahead of the game.*

Response 2

" *One thing I wish I would have known before getting into the food truck business would be all of the needed back-end permits, licenses, certifications, and insurance requirements that are all needed in order to operate. As an owner, it can get quite confusing trying to keep up with and understand all of the different mobile vending laws and to obtain all of the required credentials.*

Response 3

" *Always prepare for the unexpected; truck breaking down, selling out too soon, preparing too much. The best advice I can give is just like any other business you venture into:*

Do your homework and write a solid business plan!"

Already you can see golden information from these responses, not just for potential content, but products and services, too. But I didn't stop there.

After another week, I sent an email back to everyone who had yet to respond, the remaining 242 food truck owners, and of those, I received 42 responses back. 42! That's a 425% increase!

The riches are in the niches, but the fortune is in the follow-up.

All of the responses were so good, after the site went live I decided to publish the collection in a round-up post featuring all of the food trucks who had responded—my little way of thanking them—which later became the most-visited page on the website:

And so what was done with all of that newly found knowledge? I created a product called *How to Start a Food Truck: The Definitive Guide*, which has currently generated tens of thousands of dollars in sales and continues to make sales today.

The results also became inspiration for a lot of the other top posts on the site, including a top-ranked post on how to make a business plan for a food truck, and how to turn a food truck business into a catering company. How was I able to come up with this content even though I wasn't in the food truck industry? Like I said before, I connected with the right people in the industry who had already done it before and did the proper research. The site continues to be the top online resource available today for learning how to start and manage a food truck.

PAID TRAFFIC

If locating your target customer and reaching out to them continues to present itself as a problem (although with all of the research done, you should have no trouble finding them and sending a message to start a conversation), then you can opt for paying to advertise and get cold traffic to a webpage where you can then survey your target audience.

Facebook advertisements are the proven weapon of choice, simply because it's easy to target exactly who you're looking to reach. Advertising does, of course, require shelling out a little bit of cash to get in front of those people; and there's the additional cost of setting up a landing page, the website you're driving that cold traffic to so they can fill out that survey.

There are several other advertising platforms you could utilize to get information from your target customers, including Google AdWords and Twitter, but the setup and execution of paid advertisements is beyond the scope of this book. If you're interested in learning more about paid advertisements, I also recommend checking out material from Rick Mulready (**RICK-MULREADY.COM**) or Amy Porterfield (**AMYPORTERFIELD.COM**) too.

But like I said earlier, I crafted this book in a way where you don't have to be paying for things in order to conduct research and find the information you need.

Now, we've talked a little bit about language already, but let's get into how important it is to consider the words your target customer is using.

L:

LANGUAGE

Before I became a father, I had never held a baby in my life. To be honest, I was scared to death of holding babies because I was afraid I would break them. When my friends starting having babies and the little bundles of joy were being passed around the circle, I'd always make up an excuse or just flat out refuse. Maybe it was because I was an only child, I don't know. Then, in 2009, my wife and I had Keoni and it was like this innate part of my brain finally decided to open up and turned me into a baby-handling expert. The world works in crazy ways like that, but here's the craziest part—right from day one, I started to use baby talk.

It was weird to hear myself say things like (in a high pitched, playful kind of voice), "Hewwo my wittle boy! Hubbub bub bub bub bub!" And then pointing to their little noses, "What's that? What's that right there. Ohhhhh, daddy's got your nose!"

And trust me, it's even more weird to type this all out...but that's beside the point.

The thing I realized is that it was natural for me to talk baby talk because as parents, we try to speak our baby's language so that we can relate and engage with them more easily. Sure they are just babies and they don't necessarily understand what we're saying yet, but we try to talk like they do. Now that my son is six years old, obviously the baby talk has been put aside for more kid-like conversation (about LEGO, soccer, and pirate blasters), but it still involves language that my son can relate to, based on what words I know he knows and how he best responds to things.

When you are starting a business, one of the most important things you can do is understand the language your target customer uses to communicate. What words do they use to share their pains and struggles? How do they describe their aspirations and goals? When you can learn the language of your audience, you can more easily make a connection with them, and ultimately they begin to trust you more.

Your task in this section is to learn the language of your target customer. You've done a little bit of this while you were digging into the pains and problems of your target customer, but we're going to dive even deeper here to reveal a lot more information to help us better understand what's on their mind. To narrow down our search, we'll be looking into the three most useful kinds of words and phrases you could collect at this point:

1. Questions

2. Complaints

3. Keywords

And again, as a reminder, as you discover what words and phrases they use, insert them into your P.L.A.N. spreadsheet under the Language column.

✈

QUESTIONS

It's important to understand the specific questions your target customer is asking. After all, they are looking for answers, and if you can become the resource to provide them, whether in content format or via products or services, you're more likely to build authority and trust with your target customer as you begin to build your business and brand. Here are three ways you can quickly find what questions your target customers are asking:

Forum Search

People go to forums to ask for help. Using this specific strategy, you'll be able to quickly filter out which conversations are about a specific question from someone in your target audience.

On the Market Map you created in the last section, you will have already recorded a number of forums to research. Instead of going to each of those forums and searching through the conversations there, let's let Google do all the work for us.

STEP 1: Pick a forum and copy the URL to your clipboard.

We'll be using one of the forums we found during our fly fishing research, The Fly Fishing Forum at **HTTP://WWW.THE-FLYFISHINGFORUM.COM**

STEP 2: Type the following in Google and hit enter:

"how do I" site:
http://www.theflyfishingforum.com

This directs your search through that specific forum for any instances of the words "how do I," which are typically words people type when they are looking for help with something.

The quotations around the words you want to search for are important because it tells Google that you want them in that specific order.

STEP 3: Check out your results, and record the questions that make sense.

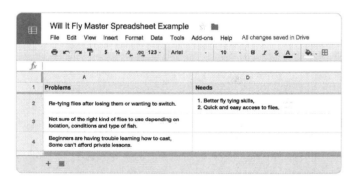

547 results. Not bad!

Other terms you could use in place of "how do I" are:

► "why is it"

► "when can I"

► "what are the"

- ► "what is the"
- ► "how come I"
- ► "need help"
- ► "please help"
- ► "I need"
- ► "help with"

You can use this same "sniper search strategy" on Google to look for any type of content on any site. Type in the words you want to look for (in quotations), followed by site: and then the website. Just like I did in the example above.

FAQs

It's harder to find your target customer posting questions on blogs because it's typically the author of that blog who is doing the posting. But, on some websites, there is one place on the site where they actually do post the common questions that their users keep asking.

An FAQ (Frequently Asked Question) page. The nice thing about FAQ pages is that we know that these are common questions. They are posted so that the author or customer service team doesn't get inundated with the same inquiry over and over again, and so that the person doing the asking can get their answer more quickly.

Just as we did to search through forums, we're now going to look for an FAQ page on the various blogs we collected in our Market Map.

STEP 1: Pick a blog and copy the URL to your clipboard.

Let's select our trusty friends over at Orvis, which we've already established as a big name in the fly fishing industry. Their URL is **HTTP://WWW.ORVIS.COM.**

STEP 2: Type the following into Google, and hit enter:

"faq" site:http://www.orvis.com

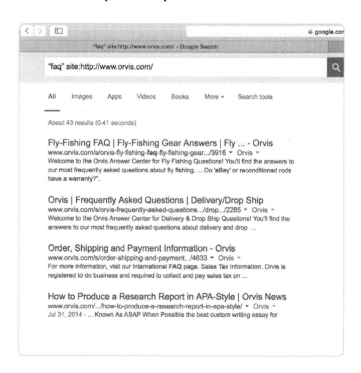

STEP 3: Click through to the FAQ page and record the questions that make sense.

Not all blogs will have FAQ pages, but I recommend you try these various phrases in your sniper search strategy to come up with similar results:

- ► "frequently asked questions"
- ► "common question"
- ► "question from"

COMPLAINTS

Complaints are some of the most useful language we can learn about our target customer. Not just because we can see what's not working and make sure we fix it in whatever solution we build, but also because you can listen to the language they use, often on a very emotional level. When you confirm their pains and struggles in a language they can relate to, it shows you're empathetic and allows you to build a stronger bond with your target customer.

Here are two strategies that you can use to find complaints from your target audience:

1. Forum Search

For this, we'll be using our trusty sniper search strategy, except using a different variation of words to find complaints.

Like before, start with the forums in your Market Map, and then locate complaints by using keywords that people use when they're unhappy:

"I hate" site:http://www.theflyfishingforum.com

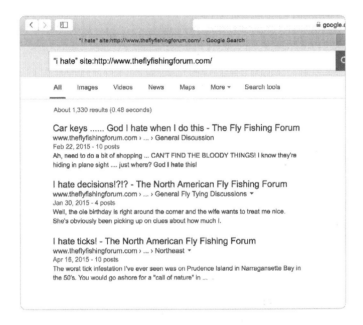

The first result from my example is actually pretty useful. It's a story about how someone lost their keys, and several others started to share their own lost key story, too. Perhaps a product for fly fisherman so they never lose their keys is needed? :)

2. Amazon Reviews

Amazon reviews are another powerful platform to look at how your target customer reacts to certain buying decisions they've made. You can then determine what their likes and dislikes are, and apply those moving forward. Here's what you do:

> ► **STEP 1:** Find a product or book on your Market Map that is sold through Amazon, and open that page.

> ► **STEP 2:** Read the 2- and 3-star reviews.

> ► **STEP 3:** Take note of any interesting complaints that people have within those reviews.

Looking at only the 2- or 3-star reviews is really important because those reviews are typically not coming from a place other than honesty. Not all, but some reviews for products are not honest. On one extreme there could be a large number of 1-star reviews from a campaign to de-rank a particular product by a competitor, and on the other hand the 5-star reviews could easily come from friends of that product owner or book publisher. That's not to say that all 1-star reviews and 5-star reviews are fake—that's definitely not the case—but for the purposes of this research we want to know what really is, and the 2- and 3-star reviews typically tell it all.

They'll say something they don't like and explain it, usually in a very thorough manner as to justify their not perfect rating, but at the same time they'll also include what is good about the product or book.

Record any interesting complaints you find in the 2- to 3-star range in Amazon for the products that you have included in your Market Map, and you'll know exactly how your target customer feels and why.

KEYWORDS

And finally, to round out the language discovery portion of our show, we're going to figure out what keywords your target audience is typing into search engines. It's important to know what those keywords are because they come from our target customer at a point when they are looking for answers, and it also gives us an opportunity to discover what potential keywords our business or service could target in our content strategy and advertising.

Keywords used to play a much larger role in the beginning stages of starting a business. There are several tools available on the market allowing a person to search through the data of hundreds of different keywords, all at the same time. That data includes things like how often a certain term is being searched for each month or the competitiveness of the sites that rank at the top of Google for those particular terms.

I used to be obsessed with searching through the fine details of this kind of data, and then building websites around the opportunistic keywords I found. Before Google was as sophisticated as it is today, it wasn't that hard to plug in a few keywords into one of these tools, get back a keyword that was deemed to be "easy," and then build a quick website to out-rank everyone else and begin making money. I've actually built websites like that before, and for a while it was the cool thing to do—mostly because it was easy.

Many people still build websites like that today, and some do end up becoming successful, but it's hardly ever because a person found the perfect keyword to target and built a website about it. The keyword alone means nothing. You need the unique, value-packed content behind it, and a deeper under-standing of who your target audience is and what they need in order to create something that's going to last.

Now, these keywords are still important to record. Like I said, they are an indicator of what your target customer is looking for and can influence what content you could eventually publish. You'll also have this handy list that you can do a lot of things with down the road once your business is established, such as advertising. We're not there yet, of course, so let's just stick with keeping it simple.

Keeping record in your P.L.A.N. spreadsheet, create a list of the keywords that your target customer is putting into various search engines.

GOOGLE RELATED SEARCHES

► **STEP 1:** Type in any keyword related to your target market, then hit enter.

► **STEP 2:** Scroll down to the bottom to locate the "Searches Related to:" section.

New to Fly? - Fly Fishing 101 | Redington Fly Fishing
www.**redington**.com/**fly-fishing**/ ▾ Redington ▾
Whether you want to know more about **fly fishing**, or you're looking for another way to enjoy the time you spend outdoors, our **Fly Fishing** 101 can help.

Searches related to redington fly fishing

redington fly fishing **reviews**	redington fly fishing **phone number**
orvis	redington fly fishing **jobs**
redington fly fishing **combo**	redington fly fishing **jackets**
redington fly fishing **vest**	**sage** fly rods

► **STEP 3:** Record those keywords into your Customer P.L.A.N. Spreadsheet

The keywords you'll find in this first set of results are usually pretty good. Remember, these are other terms people are entering in relation to that initial seed keyword. You'll get some good suggestions, but these top-level keywords are typically super-competitive. Keyword gold, especially for the purposes of content planning and understanding customer behavior, comes several levels deep. These kinds of keywords—also known as long tail keywords—are either longer keywords that include that same seed keyword, or related keywords that do not include those same words.

To get to long tail keywords that you can record into your P.L.A.N., just keep clicking through the links in the "Searches Related to:" area to start a new search using that term. Typically, the longer you go, the more long tail keywords you will find.

Here's a quick path to show you what happens after I start with a basic keyword:

FLY FISHING:

Searches related to fly fishing

fly fishing **youtube**	fly fishing **flies**
fly fishing **gear**	fly fishing **tips**
fly fishing **beginner**	fly fishing **magazine**
fly fishing **videos**	fly fishing **knots**

Goooooooooogle ›

1 2 3 4 5 6 7 8 9 10   Next

FLY FISHING BEGINNER:

Searches related to fly fishing beginner

fly fishing **casting**	fly fishing beginner **tips**
fly fishing beginner **setup**	fly fishing **knots**
fly fishing beginner **equipment**	fly fishing beginner **kit**
fly fishing **basics**	**orvis**

Goooooooooogle ›

1 2 3 4 5 6 7 8 9 10   Next

FLY FISHING BEGINNER TIPS:

Searches related to fly fishing beginner tips

fly fishing **gear for beginners**	fly fishing **equipment basics**
fly fishing **basics**	**discount** fly fishing **gear**
flyfishing	fly fishing **basic gear**
beginner fly **rods**	**how to use a fly rod**

Goooooooooogle ›

1 2 3 4 5 6 7 8 9 10   Next

By now, you should have several entries in your P.L.A.N. spreadsheet, but we have a few more important items left to help us get the full story on our target customer. Speaking of stories, in the next section, we're going to find a few.

A:

ANECDOTES

An anecdote is a short, interesting story, and they're some of the most powerful tools you can use in your business. When you are creating content and promoting products, framing it all within a story can have a massive impact on how well others relate and respond. For example, you may have noticed a number of anecdotes that I used in this book, from building paper airplanes with my son, to learning about communication from my Terminator boss. Those each came with their own lesson, but when those lessons are framed in a story they become much more relatable and memorable, and they're also a great way to hold a person's attention.

We as humans are virtually programmed right from the start to tune in and listen to stories. When we were babies, we were read stories even before we knew what was going on. Heck, stories were being told on cave walls even before formal language was created. When you hear a story, you move into the narrative world, and you can almost feel what that person or protagonist is feeling too.

Here in the final parts of this research phase, we're going to find stories about your target customer—real stories. This isn't a very common research method, but I stumbled upon it myself and have since been teaching it to others. When you can dig up stories about your target customer, you get to feel what they feel. It's a layer of personal empathy that makes you, the person who will be serving that person, more likely to pay your full attention to them. It stitches together all of the research we've already done. It makes what you do all the more real.

This isn't the same thing as creating a customer avatar, which marketers traditionally love to teach. You see, a customer avatar is made up. It's real in the sense that this persona encompasses the personality, needs, wants, and pains of real people, but it's still a fabrication. It's a generic model. I understand this methodology, however can one truly feel what a made-up avatar is feeling? I'll argue that you cannot, because your mind knows that it's not real.

Personally, what keeps me moving forward and guides my decisions in my business are the stories that I hear from my own audience. These stories help me stay connected to the person I am serving, and I try to take every opportunity I get to meet with my audience and hear their individual stories. And when I listen to their stories, I also listen for where I could have come in to help. Where in that journey did someone need a hero who wasn't there for him or her? What made them keep going, and how can I help others keep going, too?

I want you to hear the stories of real people in your target audience so that you can feel what they feel, because when you do that, you're going to easily set yourself apart from the rest, and be more committed to serving with these real people in mind.

The best place to hear a story is in person. During any one-on-one conversations that you might have with someone in your target audience, see if you can get them to tell you a story that relates to their pains and problems. A great way to set this up for yourself is to start off by saying, "Tell me a story about when you…" This simple but powerful setup will allow people to open up and for you to truly feel what they feel.

What's also helpful is that stories are shared online, and we can find them. It will take some digging, and in some niches it'll be harder to find than others, but you can use the tactics below to find some interesting stories about the people you're trying to serve.

✐

FORUM SEARCH

The forums we've collected in our Market Map have already proven themselves to be very helpful for us. Another great feature of forums is that participants feel more comfortable opening up and sharing deep, real stories with others because they're with their own people.

We'll be doing a sniper search once more, but this time with certain story-related keywords in mind.

You know the drill in terms of how to search within a site already:

"search term" site:http://www.websitename.com

Here's a list of search terms you can use with that search inquiry to help you find stories in these forums. Again, not all of them will come up with a good result, but remember, we're panning for gold here. Sometimes you're just left with dirt, and other times you see something shiny, but the more dirt you put into it the more likely you're able to find what you're looking for.

The list below is great because these are words that people will typically type after someone tells a worthwhile story. Start with:

- ➤ "amazing story"
- ➤ "great story"
- ➤ "awesome story"
- ➤ "good story"

The following don't turn up as many good results, but are still worthwhile:

- ➤ "tell you a story"
- ➤ "one time I was"
- ➤ "I remember when"
- ➤ "share a story"
- ➤ "happened to me"
- ➤ "I figured it out"

Here's one as an example:

"great story" site:http://www.theflyfishingforum.com

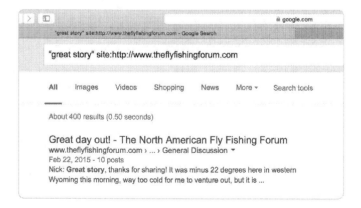

The first one down titled "Great day out!" was from a first-time fly fisherman named Nick from South Carolina. He drove two hours to fly fish on his own when he stopped at a bait shop to buy a few things and asked about the best fishing spots. Someone who was at the shop at the same time told him where he was heading and invited Nick to follow him there. Out at the fishing spot Nick, although enjoying the scenery, was struggling to learn how to cast. Just then, the guy who worked at the bait shop rolled up to check on the water clarity for a friend and noticed Nick trying to figure things out. He took five minutes to give Nick a quick casting lesson, and had Nick fishing the way he was supposed to in no time. Nick ends his story on this forum with:

" *My casts were straighter, cleaner, tighter, and a little more accurate. I never got that first trout on a fly, but I definitely got more than my 2 hours drive worth! What a great day!"*

You see this is a real story. It's not made up and we can feel what Nick felt on his first day out. You get to experience what a beginner fly fisherman is really going through on his first day on the water and you see just how much a small gesture can make a huge difference to his entire experience. And now, whenever you're speaking to a brand new fly fisherman in your posts, in your emails, or in your sales copy, you can remember Nick's story and almost imagine Nick reading your stuff. If you're creating a physical product for fly fisherman, imagine how Nick would feel using it on his first day—would he need extra help or instruction? Would he even know where to begin? If you had a service or brick and mortar store catering to fly fisherman, what's something you could do to help people like Nick have a great day on their first time out?

That's why these stories are useful, and I encourage you to find as many as possible.

AUDIO PODCAST INTERVIEWS

Podcasts have interviews, and interviews have great stories. Now, it's not as easy to find useful stories in podcasts as it was in the forums, and there will be likely fewer stories available. But if you can find an audio podcast with a story it can be even more powerful than the written ones in the forums. You get to hear the story from the person in their own voice, and if the interviewer is good, they'll dig deeper into it for you.

It's hit or miss on the podcasts in my experience, but once you find one you can read the show notes to see if it's worth listening to, and if it is, you can download it for filling in the time during your next road trip or excursion to the gym.

Again, we're going to Google to help find these, except we're going to insert a few relevant keywords all in one line, such as:

podcast "story of" "fly fishing"

This tells Google to find pages on the Internet that have the word podcast, "story of" (in that particular order), and "fly fishing" (in that particular order). Here's what we come up with:

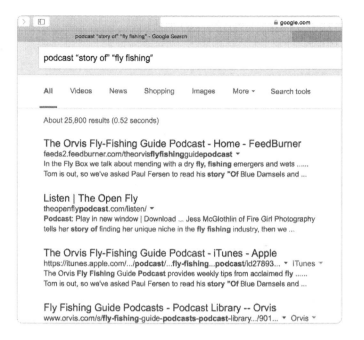

You'll have to dig through these search results, but after a few minutes I was able to find some decent stories about fly fishing that I could put into my podcast player for later.

Additionally, these real-life stories immerse you into the space in a very personal way. You'll begin to get to know people, feel like you know your way around a bit, and feel confident that you have something to offer to them.

Using these stories and the research you've done to learn about the pains and problems of your customers, in the next section you're going to determine the various needs of your target customer.

N.

NEEDS

You've put in the time and effort to learn all about your target market and the people within it, and you know it better than they even know it themselves. In this final part of the P.L.A.N, with all of the research you've done in mind, you're going to create a list of needs that your target customers have.

Before we begin, however, you must understand that a need is different than the product or business that you're potentially going to validate and build. A need is what you believe your customers require to solve a problem, and the product or business becomes the mechanism to fulfill that requirement.

For example, a problem that I discovered through my research about fly fishing is that a lot of fisherman (especially beginners) struggle to quickly re-tie flies after they lose them or when they wish to switch to a new one. In doing further analysis, which includes actual conversations with people who go fly fishing, I learned that the real pain is actually not wanting to lose the opportunity to catch the fish that's right in front of them. The more time that passes by, the more likely the fish are to move away.

There are two needs that come to mind when it comes to this particular problem. The beginner fly fisherman needs:

1. Better fly tying skills.

2. Quick and easy access to flies.

Both of these needs could become a kind of product or business! Instead of just choosing a product or business to build at random, we've got something with some good research behind it to increase the likelihood that we're building something that actually matters.

That's been the PLAN this entire time.

And what about your original idea? Well, it's likely that it has morphed into something completely different by now, or it may have completely disappeared all together now that you have new direction. For some, it could still be a viable option to test. No matter what the case may be, you're in the right place knowing that you have your target audience's problems at the root of your efforts.

Remember, a business is simply a solution to a person's problem, so we'll start this exercise in the Problems column in your P.L.A.N. sheet. To make this easier for you, we're going to temporarily hide the Language and Anecdote columns (which you can do by right-clicking on the column header and selecting "hide column") so that all you can see are the Problems and your Needs columns.

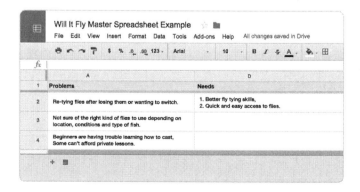

Using the problems column, determine your target audience's respective needs. Because of the way this is structured, it helps you focus on one problem at a time, which tackles a common problem a lot of entrepreneurs have: creating a solution for all problems. To start small and lean, and make it much easier for us during the validation process in Part 4, we must focus on one problem and one solution at a time.

Sometimes you won't be able to come up with a need, and that's okay. You don't have to fill out the entire matrix, but as you go along, try to think clearly about what your target customer requires in order to fight that particular problem.

By the end of this, you'll have an entire spreadsheet full of information, and somewhere within that matrix lays the root for the idea you'll be testing in Part 4! Awesome! In the next and final chapter of this book, we're going to come up with products or business solutions based on the needs that you've just found. Then, we'll pick one and see what happens.

14

ELIXIRS

S omebody once told me that the products and services we create as entrepreneurs are like elixirs—remedies or cures for certain "diseases" that are plaguing our target market. That analogy has stuck with me ever since.

In the realm of potions and medicines, an elixir is simply a concoction of stuff that already exists, mixed together in a certain way to help cure something. In a sense, that's very much what products and businesses are like. They are solutions to problems, often times a combination of stuff that already exist, made in a certain way that is more potent and effective than what's out there already. Additionally, thinking of the customer's problem like a "disease" puts into perspective exactly what we are doing here. We're not creating something for us, we're creating something they need, and if you can be the one to concoct that elixir—that cure—you'll be the one they keep coming back to, and the one they share with their friends who also have the same problem.

To finish off your customer P.L.A.N., you're going to come up with the "elixirs" that address the specific problems and needs of your target customer. These will each become a potential solution you can test and run through the customer validation method that I share with you in the next part of the book.

The solutions you come up with are like the myths from *MythBusters*. We can test them by using a specific method, at a small-scale, to prove or disprove their viability.

To start, add one more column to your P.L.A.N. spreadsheet and title it Elixir, and then one-by-one, problem-by-problem and need-by-need, come up with what you feel would be the best remedy for that problem. In some cases it'll be a physical product, in other cases it may be digital. It could be a service or a tool or piece of software—it all really depends on what it is you're trying to solve.

Like when you were mind mapping back in Chapter 7, don't let your "editor brain" get in the way here. Just let the ideas spill out based on the knowledge you have gained in this space. It's likely that you'll come up with ideas that already exist, and that's okay. It's a sign that you're on the right path, and because of the research you've done it shouldn't be too difficult to differentiate it from the other similar solutions that are already available. Again, you're at an advantage here coming in to the market after everyone else; so don't worry about those things for now. Just keep going.

After you've completed your matrix, now comes the fun part—picking one solution to test.

Great entrepreneurs test and validate one solution for one problem at a time, and now it's just a matter of picking the row in your P.L.A.N.E. that works best for you. And that's the beauty of all this. You're not just picking a customer's pain and blindly starting from there. You started with the entire map in mind, and based on everything we've done so far—the market and customer research, all the way back to the exercises we did in the

beginning to discover what kind of business worked for you—
you can now select from a menu of solutions one to pursue that
fits you. No matter which one you choose, you will be always be
serving your target customer.

At this stage, it can be tough to narrow down your selection
to one, so you may have to begin to eliminate the solutions that
aren't exciting to you. For example, maybe you're not interested
in creating any kind of service-based business and you're looking
for something a little less one-on-one with your customer. If you
see anything like that in your matrix, you can "gray out" that
particular row (don't delete it, because you may want to come
back to it later!) by highlighting it on the left hand side of your
spreadsheet, and changing the background color to a dark gray.
Boom—you've just narrowed down your selection already.

Now, not all of the elimination process will be that linear,
and it will take you some time to narrow your focus, and that's
okay. You have a lot to think about based on the research you've
already done, making sure to take note of the products that are
already serving them (or not).

You might also be wondering about your initial business idea.
Chances are your initial idea is not one that's on your current matrix. It could be, and if it is that's great; but if it's not, don't worry.
You didn't do anything wrong, and actually it validates this entire
process. You didn't spend any more time on it than necessary.

You see, ideas change and evolve over time, and you have to
expect them to do so. Ideas are just the start but through research,
discussion, and learning more about your end-user, it will shape-
shift potentially into something completely brand new.

All of the work you did to define, refine, and distill your

idea was necessary, even though it might not seem like it. Each of those exercises was a small moment of commitment to becoming an entrepreneur. The deeper you got into the process the more likely you were to follow through into your market and customer research. And now, when you eventually pick a solution, I recommend you run it through the development lab again. It'll be much easier, much more refined at the start, and you'll go in knowing that the end result is one that you know can best serve your target customer.

So to finish off this chapter, do the following:

- ► **STEP 1: Eliminate all but one row and one solution on your matrix.** You should end up with one solution for one pain/problem.

- ► **STEP 2: Sit on that idea for a day.** Think about it in your normal everyday life and let it sink in. Pay attention to how it makes you feel, and be sure to keep a notepad with you, because your brain is going to be in rapid-fire creation mode during that process. Write down anything and everything that comes to mind.

- ► **STEP 3: Conduct a second mind mapping exercise with your new target solution as the focal point.** After a 10-minute brainstorming session, remove anything and everything that does not relate to solving the one target pain/problem corresponding to that solution. If it doesn't 100% support the act of solving that pain, remove that note from your mind map.

► **STEP 4: One page, one paragraph, one sentence.**

We're going to wait to talk about your idea with others, because that's what we're going to do in the next part of the book, with a little hidden agenda in mind. We're going to have our target customers validate our idea for us at the same time.

Great work! You've done more work in this section than you've done before. I didn't say any of this would be easy, but hopefully you're starting to see how this is all coming together. Be proud, because not everyone gets to this part. Many drop out earlier in the process because they are afraid to do the work required to make things happen, but you're obviously not one of those people.

In Part 4, we're going to enter the flight simulator where you'll actually be putting your focused business solution to the test with your target customer, and potentially even getting paid for it. I hope you're as excited as I am. Once you're ready, flip to the next page. I'll see you there.

FLIGHT
SIMULATOR

"Intuition and experience are poor predictors of which products and businesses will be profitable...To get an accurate indicator of commercial viability, don't ask people if they would buy—ask them to buy. The response to the second is the only one that matters."

—TIM FERRISS, *THE 4-HOUR WORK WEEK*

15

THE SILENT HERO

I remember watching *Apollo 13* when I was little. Not the *actual* Apollo 13 mission—that was 45 years ago when I was negative 12 years old—but the 1995 film starring Tom Hanks, Bill Paxton and Kevin Bacon. I was positive 12 years old when that hit the theaters, and after watching it twice, it shot up the ranks to become one of my all-time favorite movies.

I think that's where my love of all things space started. I vividly remember a few scenes from the movie that really stood out to me. Being a 12-year-old boy, of course, there's the one when Tom Hanks pees into a tube and then presses a button called "urine dump" to release it into space. Another scene was when CO_2 was rising to dangerous levels and the engineers at Mission Control had to quickly come up with a solution using only materials that were available to the astronauts in order to save their lives. And then there were the various scenes in the flight simulator, where the astronauts trained for procedures in a simulated space environment, typically failing over and over again until they figured out the right way to do something.

The astronauts and the entire crew down on Earth were the celebrated heroes of the story, but in my opinion the flight simulator was pretty important, too. Without the simulator and its capability to allow the astronauts and engineers to hone in on what was going to work, their chances of surviving in space would have been zero.

Simulation is an essential part of flight training, whether we're talking about spaceships, 747s, or Cessnas. Pilots have to spend countless hours in a flight simulator before they're allowed to walk aboard a plane and turn left instead of right.

In this chapter you're going to enter your own flight simulator, testing your idea and validating it on a small scale so that you can make sure it works. Along the way, you'll be able to make adjustments and fine-tune your approach so that you can be ready and confident before you start counting down to the real launch.

Different solutions lend themselves to different validation techniques, and we'll be going over all of them in this chapter, including how and why each of them work, and a step-by-step process you can follow. You'll also get to see real life examples of how different people tested their own business ideas before launching and going full-scale, all of whom had paying target customers before the solution was even built.

So what are we waiting for? Let's get started and learn about the principles of validation and how it can work for us.

16

PRINCIPLES OF VALIDATION

ʠ ʠ I'll believe it when I see it."

That was the line my mom would always mutter under her breath when I promised to clean my perpetually messy room.

I didn't know this at the time, but my mom was giving me a very important lesson in validation. What someone says they're going to do, and what they actually end up doing can be completely different, so you need more than just words in order to count on them. Sorry, mom!

The worst mistake you can make when building your business is the one that I made in 2010 when I was trying to build two premium WordPress plugins and lost $15,000 in the process. I tried keeping everything secret. You don't have to reveal your idea to the entire world, but as we learned in the Development Lab, speaking to a few people about what you're up to is vital. I would have quickly learned that I was heading down the wrong direction and spending cash where it didn't need to be spent had I listened to that advice.

The second worst mistake that you can make is building your business based on someone's word that it's something they would buy or use. Like my mom taught me, what people say and what they end up doing can be completely different, and in the world of entrepreneurship, the following is what you need to know when it comes to what other people say:

Listen to others, but trust your numbers.

It's easy to say something, but it means a whole lot more when people speak with their actions instead.

In order to be confident in your decision to move forward with your idea, you need people to step up and actually take action. There are varying degrees of action, and with each comes a certain level of confidence and validation, but you need people to stop talking, and start doing.

Pre-build validation isn't new, but there was one person who put it on the map. Tim Ferriss, author of the bestselling book *The 4-Hour Work Week*, revealed a strategy in the section of his book called "Testing the Muse." In it, he gave two examples of micro-testing products for two hypothetical businesses: one selling "How to Yoga" DVDs and the other French sailor shirts.

Tim's method of validation was using Google AdWords, an advertising platform, to gauge interest by placing ads for these products to determine whether or not there was a demand. People would see these ads, click through to the sales page, and click the buy now button to make a purchase. There was no product, of course, so the user would be prompted with an "out of stock" message, but because every click was tracked, it was easy to see if people actually wanted to buy these products, or not.

A lot of people did exactly what Tim taught and have started muse businesses of their own, and my goal is that you'll be able to do the same thanks to the validation strategies shared in this book too.

There's one common question when it comes to validation that we have to address before we move on:

Is there a way to know with 100% certainty that my idea will become successful?

The honest answer is no, because you will never know for sure until you actually build the thing and see for yourself. There are so many other factors involved, from the timing to the build and the execution. Great ideas, even ones that have been validated in some way, require great execution in order to succeed.

What we're doing here is validating whether or not your idea *could* become a success. Finding out that it *could* is a huge realization, a big-time motivator that will have you executing faster than ever to turn that small-scale test into a full-scale business.

You've been going through an iterative process in just the time you've been reading this book. Stage after stage, you have evaluated your idea and then made a conscious decision to either keep going, or re-work what you just did and try again. With each step forward you built your confidence on the work that you had just done.

The validation stage is a part of that overall process. You will execute, evaluate and make a decision. If it turns out you have indeed validated your idea and your target customers are taking action, then you can move onto the next step and build it out.

The real question we have to answer is this:

How do we define success within the scope of validation?

The purpose of testing anything is to answer the simple, yet crucial question: **does the idea work?**

Whether it works or it does not, **successful validation**

also comes with understanding why things happened the way they did. This knowledge will bring you closer to your ultimate goal.

There are a lot of other side-benefits to validation, which will help you become a smarter entrepreneur:

1. You receive invaluable feedback from the actions people take.

Even if what you do fails, even if your pre-sale fails to generate even one purchase, you will still end up with a clear direction to (not) move forward. You can reassess what went wrong and tweak things until they work. Gone are the times when we think, "If you build it, they will come"—that is a dream, and a false one at that. However, Grant Baldwin (**GRANTBALDWIN. COM**), an entrepreneur, public speaker and digital marketer once explained on my blog why validation and getting people involved early in the process is important.

> " *The common model for building products is we have an idea… we go into our workshop to make it….we emerge back into civilization…we shout from the rooftops what we've made…. we wait and hope we hit the mark and people actually give us money. And sometimes this can work. But sometimes it can lead to a huge flop that could have been prevented. By getting others involved early in the process, you can get actual feedback from real customers and build not what you think they want but what they actually want."*

2. You get early experience selling something.

Pre-selling to validate your product is a great way to train yourself for bigger, more profitable launches down the road. Once things start to take motion, momentum starts to build and you gain the confidence required to sell. Confidence is an important key to succeeding in any sales, because if you aren't confident in the launch and the product, it's likely that you're going to distill a lack of confidence in your selling techniques. Buyer confidence will decrease as a result. You really have to believe in what you're doing, or else no one else will. Make a few sales in the beginning, even before you build, and your confidence levels go through the roof.

3. You can get money in your pocket upfront.

Obviously, getting cash up front for something is great. You can begin to see an income from your potential work, you get cash to help you pay for the development of whatever it is that you're creating, and it could also help you convince that person that has been telling you this isn't going to work to, well...try and have more support for you.

NOTE: *it's never worth trying to convince someone who doesn't believe in what you're doing to change his or her mind. Let your results speak for you, and surround yourself with like-minded people who support you, can lift you up, and help you by holding you accountable without putting you down.*

4. It will motivate you to follow through and get things done!

Nothing else lights the fire under your butt more than when you see that people are actually interested in what you have to offer, so much so that they'd pay you for it before it's even made. That proof will motivate you to put in the work required to follow through and deliver on your promises.

Part of the struggle a lot of people have when doing their own thing as an entrepreneur is that we're so used to getting paid X dollars for putting in X hours of work. When we are working hard up front for nothing we think we're not getting anywhere, and we begin to psych ourselves out because we're not seeing any money coming in the door yet. But, if you validate your product or service and can get paid up front, you'll be incredibly motivated to see that what you're working on is actually working. It can charge you up to continue finishing your project. Beyond the money that can come in as a result of pre-ordering, the fact that there are actually people on the other end who have trusted you with their money will get you moving, because you will not want to let those people down.

Are you ready to check out how validation works? Let's get right into it on the next page.

17

THE VALIDATION METHOD

As we stated earlier, validation is not based on someone telling you they would buy, like, read, consume, watch or listen to something you create. Validation is based on certain actions they take. The basic formula for validation follows this exact sequence:

- ► **STEP 1: Get in front of an audience.**

- ► **STEP 2: Hyper-target.**

- ► **STEP 3: Interact and share your solution.**

- ► **STEP 4: Ask for the transaction.**

Each of these components play a specific role in the validation process, so let's define what each of these are and then we'll put them all together. Although this is broken down into four steps, I don't want to discount the fact that validation requires hard work. It does. But, that's why you're here and not the other person who is just dreaming and waiting for things to happen. You're making them happen. So let's get started…

STEP 1: Get in front of an audience.

You need to get access to an audience of people in your market. Without that audience, you can't properly validate, and this is where a lot of people stumble with validation.

A lot of the validation material I've come across reveals some very attractive techniques that help you understand if people are interested in your solution or not, but they don't get into how to find those people in the first place. Many of them assume you already have a following or an email list, but unfortunately everyone else is left in the dark.

If you've built an audience and have a following already, then great! You already have what you need to move onto the next step, no matter how big or small the size of your platform.

If you don't have an audience yet, don't worry. That audience you need doesn't have to be one that you own or build yourself. You just need to get access to an audience, and there are several different ways to do that.

TARGETED ADVERTISING

There are several different advertising platforms available that you can use to serve ads and get in front of your target market to gauge the interest they have in what you have to offer. Using Google AdWords is the method Tim Ferriss mentioned in *The 4-Hour Work Week*, however other advertising platforms like Facebook and Twitter allow you to hone in even further on the people you are serving ads to.

Of course, you will have to pay for the ads. The pricing

depends on a number of factors but it's almost always based on the number of clicks on your ads (pay-per-click). If your ads don't get any clicks, then you don't pay anything. At the same time, however, you'd validate that no one was clicking on your ads.

If no one clicks on your ad, does that mean your idea doesn't work? Not necessarily. It just means the ad wasn't working, which is the potential problem with this particular method. Maybe the ad was off-putting or it just didn't make sense, which would give you a false reading on how valid your idea is.

If you run ads and they do work, then that's a good sign. Keep note of that ad and the language that you used to earn those clicks—they work. But, does that validate your idea? Not yet, because it just simply validates that advertisement. True validation comes later, but let's get into more methods for getting in front of an audience if you don't have one yet, or if you'd like to expand the one you already have.

Where do people land when they click on these ads? It can be to a variety of places, including a landing page, a survey, or even a webinar registration. More on the follow-up in Step 2 of the validation method. For now, let's keep going on how else we can get in front of an audience.

✈

PRIVATE TARGETED ADVERTISING

We're still talking about advertising here, which means you'll likely have to pay for these ads too, but instead of being served in front of a targeted audience on Google, Facebook, or Twitter, you're serving these ads on specific websites where you know your target audience already exists.

In this case, you deal directly with the owner of a website to come up with a deal to place an ad somewhere. There's a lot more room for creativity here. That ad could be a banner advertisement, a mention in an email broadcast or blog post, a social media mention, or anything else you can think of. It could even be a combination of all of the above.

The idea is to place yourself in front of an audience that already exists on a website that is not yours, and because that ad or mention is on a website with some authority in the space, you're going to have a lot more confidence in the results that come back your way.

So where do you find these websites or website owners? Lucky you, you already have the Places and People listed in your Market Map from Chapter 12! If you haven't done so already, strike up a conversation and build a real relationship with these people first before asking for potential ad placement on the site—and when you get to that point in the conversation, I'd recommend being very honest about why you're doing it.

Like before, if the ads seem to convert, that's great news but it doesn't tell the whole story yet. What matters is what happens next, but for now at least you know you've got the messaging right. If the ads do not convert, it doesn't mean the solution is bad, it just means that the way it was presented didn't work, and you can easily make adjustments from there if needed.

✐

GUEST POSTING

A guest post is an article that you write that you publish on another website. This can be one of the most powerful ways to start the validation process for your solution because instead of advertising, you're providing value, being endorsed by the owner of the site, and you're starting to build a relationship with people who get to know you through your article who could become interested in what else you have to offer.

This doesn't cost any money, but what it will require is some relationship building with the owner of the website where you'd like to guest post. Similar to the previous example, you can start with your Market Map to determine which websites to target, and then determine what kind of article to write for that particular site from there.

⌁

FORUMS

Do you remember those forums we found in our Market Map? Those are platforms where your target audience already exists, which gives you an opportunity to get in front of that audience too with a very low barrier to entry. Instead of going through a site owner the way you'd have to do in order to guest post, you can simply join the forum and write a post of your own.

That being said, if the first impression you offer them is an introduction that includes a massive call to action, you're not going to receive a very warm welcome. Any community, both online and offline, is going to be very protective of their space, so you have to spend a little bit of time building a rapport with the people there. Show them that you have value to provide to the group.

Pick two or three of the forums in your database and spend at least a week posting valuable information and responding to questions before asking for anything in return. During this time, you could get even deeper into your market research, and pinpoint a few individuals with whom you'd like to strike up a conversation.

There was an architecture forum that was really popular at the time that I was building my business, and within that forum was a sub-forum that was all about the LEED exam. I discovered it after I began building my business but I didn't talk about my business at all until another forum user asked me about it a few weeks later. When I first introduced myself, I said I was simply there as a resource to help people and I began answering as many questions as I could and participated in as many discussions as possible. I ended up becoming good friends with a few of the power-users in the group and eventually the news came out that I was building my website, and the forum became a huge resource for traffic, feedback, and validation as I moved forward in my business and created new products.

GROUPS

Similar to Forums, there are tons of groups on social media sites like Facebook and LinkedIn related to your market that you could treat in a very similar way. These are existing communities where you don't want to come in and immediately ask people to do something for you. Here, you join the conversations and build relationships, and naturally you'll gain authority and earn the right to ask people to take action in one way or another.

I suggest starting with three to five groups and participating daily for a week before asking for any favors of any kind. Share items that are relevant to the group and provide value in every post. When you do this, you will get noticed and you will build trust with those who are there.

I know a lot of people in my own Facebook groups that I manage who have "climbed the ranks" within those groups because of the value that they've provided others. Many of them are now admins for those groups and help manage the conversations and keep the groups clean of spam. Thanks, admins! You rock!

THE "POSTER CHILD" FORMULA

This is a strategy that was coined by Bryan Harris of **VIDEOFRUIT.COM**. He describes a poster child as, "the example that every teacher uses to teach his or her students. She is the model student, always does her homework and makes everyone else look bad for not doing theirs. As much as you hated that kid in school, it's time for you to become that person."

When implemented correctly, you can get featured by influencers on their platforms all without having to write a guest post. Bryan has used this several times in the past, and I've even used it, too. It works.

Every influencer wants to show their audience that what they are teaching or sharing with the world is making an impact, and if you become their "poster child"—a case study of someone who has used that content or a product and has benefited from it in some way—there's a good chance that you will be shared and be able to get in front of a targeted audience. If anything, it will help you build a strong relationship with that influencer and could open up even more opportunities for you down the road.

This happened to me when my LEED exam site was taking

off and I started sharing that information with the community at Internet Business Mastery Academy, a course and community that I got involved with when I was just starting out. The site's owners, Jeremy Frandsen and Jason Van Orden, later made me into a case study, complete with filming my story and sharing it with their entire email list.

You have a list of websites and influencers already, it's just a matter of being smart about the ones you target, and what you can apply and share with that person after you get results. It may be wise to go through each of their websites first if you haven't already, and see which ones are already highlighting his or her audience members in some way.

This is yet another way to get in front of an audience if you don't have one already. You really have no excuse even if you haven't already built a following. We'll talk about what to do when you get in front of that audience later in this chapter, but let's keep going with strategies to get in front of an audience. After all, the more items you have to select from the menu, the more likely there will be that one strategy that looks appetizing to you.

THE DEREK HALPERN STRATEGY

Derek Halpern is a good friend of mine who blogs at **SOCIALTRIGGERS.COM**. He started his blog in early 2011 to help people make the connection between psychology and business. It's one of my favorite sites because the content is always incredibly actionable and helpful. How we came to meet (I didn't realize until later) was part of an overall strategy that Derek used to get in front of large audiences and quickly get his name out there.

Even after just getting to know him, I was mentioning his name and linking to him all over my site, and so were several other influencers. All because Derek reached out and immediately provided me with some value. Here's what he did.

After a quick introduction, he shared a quick tip with me to help me increase the number of email subscribers I was getting each day—something I really wanted to happen—and I implemented that strategy and saw immediate results from it. He had asked for nothing in return, and of course being super thankful, I sent him an email to show him the results and see if there was anything I could do for him.

He then offered to do a free, full-site review for any of my websites, and I chose to have him continue to critique and review **SMARTPASSIVEINCOME.COM**. His information was so good that I decided to create an entire video featuring Derek's advice and sharing that on my YouTube channel and blog.

He did this for several other people who also shared his work in some way, shape, or form. He was able to get in front of incredibly large audiences, with the blessing of an influencer in his target market, in a relatively short period of time.

When you provide value to others, more often than not, especially if they get results from what you share, they are going to want to find ways to pay you back for it—especially if they get results.

$$\diagdown$$

OFFLINE AUDIENCES

Validating an idea online is helpful because you can reach large audiences in a relatively short period of time and better track your results along the way. But getting in front of a live audience in person can help you gauge interest about a particular topic, too.

You could try to land a speaking gig at an upcoming conference that you know your target audience attends, which can help you not only start a conversation with these people, but also allow you to begin to make a name for yourself in the space. When I started speaking I spoke for free simply to get the experience before I started charging for my time on stage. Each of those speaking opportunities became an amazing way to get people interested in who I was and what else I had to offer. Of course, you'll want to bring something relevant and value-packed on the stage, but it's good practice, for sure. Plus, now that you know this is a target market of interest to you, it would be beneficial for you no matter what your solution may be.

How can you land a speaking opportunity if no one knows who you are? Lots of conferences take applications and if you can present a good idea you could potentially be asked to speak. Also, I wouldn't hesitate to reach out specifically to the conference team to introduce yourself and express interest in speaking, too.

When I started speaking and wanted to speak more, a lot of the opportunities I had came about through the relationships I had built with other speakers at those events, so you can utilize your network if you have any connections there. You could also offer to be a part of or even lead a panel made up of a number of different speakers to talk about a particular topic of interest to your target audience. And the more you speak, the more speaking opportunities you will get, and it's an amazing way to get in front of an audience and have them learn more about who you are.

If speaking at a conference isn't going to work for whatever reason, you can still meet your target audience in person outside of the presentation rooms and in the hallways and net-working events that conferences usually put into their schedules. You now know how important it is to speak to people in person about your idea, and putting yourself in a conference situation with opportunities to meet your target audience in person can be a big win.

As you can probably tell by now, a lot of these strategies are ones that you can take with you into the future as you begin to build your business, so definitely keep these in mind for later. For now, however, as you begin to validate your idea, the purpose of these strategies is to help you get in front of your target audience to inspect issues related to your business solution.

Of course, you could start a platform of your own like a blog, podcast, or video channel to slowly build an audience and authority from there, but these strategies will help you gain traction much faster and learn about how your idea works (or doesn't) much sooner.

The validation process I'm teaching is a very iterative process, meaning it's simple but broken down into chunks so each one of these stages becomes a validation point itself. This first step, for example, validates whether or not you can get in front of your target audience. The other steps don't matter until this happens, so you can narrow your focus on this first step before you move onto the next part of the process. If for whatever reason it's not working out, then you can find out what those reasons are, reiterate this particular step until you get it right.

Before we get into Step 2 of the validation method, now's the time to talk about something that has become very popular during recent years to help people and businesses validate their product ideas and get paid for it even before building it out.

CROWDFUNDING PLATFORMS

Crowdfunding is an all-in-one validation method that allows you to share an upcoming project in a marketplace where there are existing users who, if they are interested, will pledge money to support you and your campaign in exchange for the future build of the project and various pledge rewards that you offer along with it. Typically, the more a person pledges to your campaign, the bigger the reward or giveaway will be.

Platforms like KickStarter (**KICKSTARTER.COM**) and Indiegogo (**INDIEGOGO.COM**) have become massively popular over the past few years, and tens of thousands of projects and ideas are concurrently showcased hoping to raise enough money to get their businesses off the ground. Many companies got their start with the help of raising money on these platforms, and I included it here in this section because it is indeed a way to get in front of an audience and validate an idea, even if you don't already have a following.

The benefits of using a crowdfunding platform to validate your idea are:

1. **You get the exposure from the existing audience that those platforms have.**

2. **They are trusted marketplaces where people are comfortable using the platform to pledge and pre-order items.**

3. **The platforms enable you to communicate with people about your project, even after**

the pledge period ends so you can keep them informed about the project build and other news.

4. **You can begin to build a following.**

5. **It's possible to generate a sizable amount of income, even beyond what your pledge goal might be.**

Now, this might sound like a dream come true, and so you might be thinking, "Why are we wasting time with the rest of this book? Why not just get on KickStarter and validate my idea there?" Well, here's why:

1. **All crowdfunding platforms take a cut of your overall pledge earnings;** that's how they survive. That's not terrible because you're paying for the service, but there's more.

2. **You have to have a good campaign page.** This means high-quality video, superb copywriting, and compelling pledge rewards. This isn't something you can just put together overnight. The quality of your campaign page reflects the quality of your product, and so by adding this kind of platform into your validation strategy you introduce another failure point, where if the campaign didn't work out you wouldn't know if it was because the product was bad, or because your campaign was off.

3. **Fulfillment of pledge items has taken over some people's lives.** There are now businesses that

exist specifically to help companies fulfill pledge rewards on crowdfunding platforms, which tells you just how much extra work this will take, and how many hours it may remove from your time with the actual business you want to create. Let's say, for example, you decide to offer a T-shirt to those who pledge $50 to your campaign. Do you have a t-shirt company in mind to make those shirts? What about the design? Plus, there's all the different sizes, and then shipping, too. It's a lot to think about, which is why I bring it up here.

And the big one:

4. **It's not a fully controlled small-scale experiment anymore.** It's something that could potentially grow bigger than you can keep up with, and if you truly want to validate your idea first, I suggest starting small and using the methods in this book. Then, if it checks out and makes sense for you and your business, it might make sense to use KickStarter or another platform like it to launch it at full scale, raising funds to expand and grow more quickly. By then, you'll have some paying customers already that could help make your promotional videos even better with testimonials, and your product will be better by then because you'll have time to get feedback from your initial set of customers. Plus, if that campaign doesn't work out, you'll know it wasn't because the product wasn't what people wanted.

Let's keep moving…

Now, once you get in front that audience, no matter what method you choose, the next step is to get people in that audience to "raise their hands."

STEP 2: Hyper-target (a.k.a. The Hand Raise).

Once you gain access to an audience, whether that's through one of the strategies mentioned in Step 1, or through the audience that you've already built, the next phase in the validation process is to hyper-target. This means getting people in that larger target market to self-identify as someone who wants or needs your particular solution.

I like to metaphorically describe this phase as getting a targeted portion of that audience to "raise their hand." Why a hand raise? Because raising one's hand is simple. It takes almost no energy to perform, but there is so much meaning behind it.

A hand raise signals "me!" or "yes!" As a public speaker, I've learned what an amazing tool a hand raise can be within a presentation. A lot of speakers will start a question with the phrase "by a show of hands," or "please raise your hand if," in order to quickly and easily survey an audience and identify certain groups within it without much effort from the audience itself.

Using this methodology, you can begin to identify the portion of an overall target market with which you can take the next steps. The truth is that it's very unlikely that 100% of any general target market will be completely interested in your solution, so it's important to validate only with those for whom your solution would be suited.

For example, if your target market is fly fisherman, and you have a product specifically suited for beginners, not everyone who goes fly fishing will be interested in your particular solution. In order to properly validate your idea, you need to at least discover who the beginner fly fisherman is. Depending on what your idea is, you may need to narrow down your search even more. Let's say your solution helps fisherman discover what their first set of gear should be. Well, then you need to find those who are not only beginners, but those who have yet to purchase their gear.

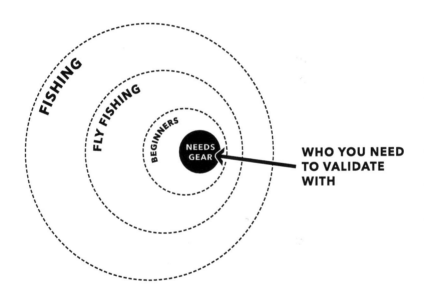

Before we get into specific methods to get a focused segment of an audience to "raise their hand," it's important to know that you're not yet presenting your actual solution at this point. If you were to ask everyone if they were interested in your solution, you're going to get a "no" from several people simply because not everyone will need that solution. That's why it's important to filter those people out through this process. By doing so, you will present your solution only to those who would find it useful.

Furthermore, as before, we're separating each part of the validation process so we can understand what's happening during each phase. If you were to share your solution to everyone and it didn't work, you wouldn't know if it's because people aren't interested in it, or because the people who your solution is made for simply aren't there. Let's see if they're there first, and then move onto the next step.

In order to get a target segment of the audience to "raise their hand" and express interest, you must first ask them a question or propose a relevant scenario that elicits a "yes" or "that's me" response from them. This also becomes the first step in a "yes-ladder" that you're creating, which is a psychological technique where you start with small positive responses that lead to an increased likelihood of drawing out a positive response from a bigger ask down the road. This gives you the best chance of positively validating your solution, as opposed to simply asking what they think about it from the start.

There are lots of different methods we can use to get a hand raise from our audience. A comment or response is typically the easiest way for people to say "yes," such as in a forum, a blog post or social media post. A click on a link is another way to gauge interest, such as ones within an email, blog post, or even an advertisement. Other forms of a "hand raise" include downloading something, subscribing to an email list, sending you a personal email, or even picking up the phone and calling you. I'll give you specific examples in context, both for those who are just starting out and those who already have a following in the next chapter. For now, let's keep moving along and learn about Step 3 of the validation process, which is all about interacting and sharing your solution with the hand raisers.

STEP 3: Interact and share your solution.

After you've discovered who your prospects are, it's time to interact with those people directly. You're not quite presenting your solution yet, but you're really close. The idea here is to start to engage with the people who have signaled interest.

Because this is interactive, this is a great opportunity for you to learn how to get comfortable talking to others, and to sell comfortably without it being too risky. Actually, everything you've done so far has been done to minimize the risk, and when you interact with your prospects, you have to ask yourself, "What's the worst that can happen?" It's never going to be as bad as you think, and remember, even if people say they aren't interested in what you have to offer, that's still a win for you, because you can learn why and use that information moving forward.

The reason I bring this up is because when I first started as an entrepreneur, I was deathly afraid to interact with people when I knew I was going to eventually ask for money. You've already learned how to talk to people about your idea, but adding the pitch element to it scares a lot of people, like it did to me. A lot of my worry went away over time simply because I just kept doing it (which is why it's important we start now if this is something you feel will be an issue for you). However, I also realized that if I have a product that can make a difference in another person's life, or if I'm striking a deal with a company that I know is going to help my audience, it's my duty to have that conversation and it's my right to ask to get paid for providing that value. If you have a product you believe in, you would be doing your target customer, and yourself a disservice by not selling it to get it in the hands of others.

All selling starts with the relationship, which means that you have to make sure that you begin by getting the person on the other end to know, like, and trust you. This is one of the benefits of building an audience first (which again, does not happen overnight) because you earn that trust with your audience over time. It also justifies why it's important to make sure you don't start asking for things the moment you join a new group or forum, but rather take the time to deliver value and allow people to get to know you first. If you've done everything the way you were supposed to, you will have already provided value to the people you reach out to in some way. In the next chapter you'll see how different people across different niches started out by getting in front of audiences and providing value first before asking for anything in return. It doesn't take long, but it must be done or else you'll be ignored.

There are several methods you can choose to directly interact with your prospects. One-on-one is always going to be the most effective, but there are a lot to ways to interact in this manner. The following one-on-one methods are ranked from most effective (top) to the least effective (bottom), but also most time consuming in the same order.

- ► In person
- ► A video call, like a Google Hangout or Skype conversation
- ► A phone call
- ► A private message (i.e. on a forum or social media channel)
- ► A direct one-on-one email

You'll have to strike a balance based on what works for you, but also what works for your prospects based on how you're finding them.

There are also methods you can use to interact with a large number of your prospects at the same time. These methods can save you time, but they take a little more work up front to set up. If you've already built a following and have earned trust from your audience, these can work very well, especially if you have an email list. Again, these are ranked from most effective (top) to the least effective (bottom).

- A live stream or webinar with chat functionality
- A live stream or webinar without chat functionality
- An email broadcast
- A web page with an explainer video
- A web page with text and images only
- Morse code

No matter which method you choose to interact with your prospect, there are three things you must do first before you present your solution, each of which will help your prospect get to know, like, and trust you.

1. Take a minute to learn about them first (while also confirming they are in the right place).

After thanking them for their time, you can begin by simply asking a question or two to learn more about your prospect, which serves double duty for you. First, people love to talk about themselves, and when given the opportunity, they will do just that. Open up the floor to allow them to share what it is they do and try to keep it related to the topic or market they are in. This will also make them feel more comfortable and they open up even more later in the conversation.

This can be done both in a one-on-one scenario, and in a live streaming group setting with chat functionality. If you're in a group setting, asking questions to get to know your audience is a great strategy to keep people engaged and interested while you learn about who you're speaking to at the same time.

In addition to a normal greeting and thanking them for their time, you could ask a question like, "So how long have you been doing _____?" That question's answer could lead to a few other natural follow-up questions from there. Again, this is you building a relationship with this person in a very short period of time, so keep it about them first.

Second, these questions help you and your prospect know they are in the right place. The prior question I shared does this already, but you can hone in on one that makes sure it relates to the problem your solution solves, which gives you a perfect segue into who you are and why you're having this conversation in the first place.

For example, if your product was for beginner fly fisherman who have yet to get their own gear, you could ask something like, "What made you get interested in fly fishing?"

And don't forget about the language you've learned about this audience in your Customer P.L.A.N. This is one of those moments where that information can come in handy.

> **QUICK TIP:** *If you're planning on speaking to prospects one-on-one, make sure you refer to them by name right from the start. Additionally, if you have some time before your calls or interactions, try to get to know the person via their social media profiles and find any connections that you may have. Perhaps you went to the same school or you're both parents. These little connections can speed up the relationship building process quite fast in a conversation.*

2. Qualify yourself.

From there, you want to make sure you qualify yourself. This means sharing a little bit about who you are, but also why they should continue to listen to you.

After this super quick introduction, you'll want to talk about why you're the one doing this. Your own personal accolades are not as important as why you are serving them, so keep that in mind during this part of the conversation. It's not about you, it's about what you can do for them.

A quick story about how you came about wanting to serve this audience can work well, too.

3. Be honest about what you're up to.

And finally, before getting into sharing your solution, it's important that you're honest with the person on the other end as to why you're having this conversation in the first place. In my opinion, it's always best to be able to reveal things yourself first rather than having someone else find out later, so I'd be completely upfront about the fact that you're hoping to get their honest feedback on something you believe will help them that isn't built or available yet, but that you will create and sell it if there is enough interest.

Sharing this puts your prospect in the right mindset for this experiment. They'll trust you even more because you were upfront about the fact that it's not built yet and you're currently in the process of validating your idea. Furthermore, they'll continue thinking about your solution and how it's a good fit (or not) for them into the rest of the conversation, which is exactly what you want.

All of the above should take no longer than two or three minutes. It's quick. Again, you don't want to waste your time, or that of the other person. Plus, if you're doing these on a one-on-one basis, you want to get through as many people as possible to get more accurate results.

After you re-qualify the person through this quick conversation, it's time to reveal your solution.

THE PITCH

At this point, you're not asking for any kind of payment yet, but you are selling your idea to the person on the other end to determine whether or not this is a solution that solves their pain or problem that makes sense to them. How you describe your solution to your prospect will be based heavily on what you've done in your mind mapping exercise and what you've written on your "one page, one paragraph, one sentence" exercise, and I would lead with that one focused sentence.

If possible and relevant, you could also share a prototype of your solution with your audience. This is obviously difficult to do if you're on a phone call so it's not always possible, but I like the idea of having some initial version of your solution available to see because it makes this all the more real.

Don't be scared about the word prototype though, it's not anything close to what the final product will become and it doesn't even have to be anything that actually works. But, it's something visual beyond words that you can share with your audience that reveals your solution. When people hear the word prototype, they usually think of a first version of something physical, but that doesn't always have to be the case, and it usually isn't. Whether your solution is a physical product, a digital product, or even a service of some kind, you should have a preliminary model of it to share with your hyper-targeted audience in some shape or form. If it's a software product, for example, your mock-up could simply be a wireframe or rough sketch of the interface. If it's a book, perhaps you list the outline of it. If it's a physical product and you don't have access to a hands-on prototype, maybe it's a 3D rendering or sketches of it. Whatever you need to make sure your prospect understands how this will help them is what you should create. Don't get "asset happy" or create assets just for the sake of decoration or adornment, and don't worry about the quality either. Sometimes, the more rough, the better—as long as the ideas come across.

So how much interest should you have in order to call this a success?

We're almost able to answer that question, but not yet. Because we're still taking people's word for it, we can't be sure from what has already been said if our idea is good enough to move forward with at this point—but if it's not good it'll be completely obvious, as we've mentioned several times already.

In the next and final step of the validation process, we'll be asking people to say yes not with their words, but with a payment. Yes, you'll be asking your prospects to pay money ahead of when the product is actually built. The way you pitch and how you frame this matters, so let's get right into the final step, along with specifics on what makes this a success.

STEP 4: Ask for the transaction.

Asking for a payment before you build your product might feel uncomfortable to you, but again if you're honest about this with your prospect, you'll have nothing to worry about. Furthermore, paying for something ahead of time is something people are a lot more comfortable doing with platforms like KickStarter and Indiegogo on the rise. At this point, you've got your prospect's attention. You've provided value and you've shared what your plan is. The next step is to get those who are interested to validate with a transaction.

Now, if you're pitching in a group setting you'll want to provide your call to action immediately after you share your solution. For example, if you've got a number of people attending a webinar, you should provide a web address where they can pay to be a part of the early adopter program *after* you provide value and share what you're planning to do. Later in this chapter I'll share the tools you can use to make this happen.

If you're in a live one-on-one setting, you have a couple options. You could ask for the transaction immediately, or you could follow up a day later. It can be done both ways.

Here's an example email or message that you could send to a prospect you shared your solution with earlier:

Hey Jim, thanks again for taking the time to chat with me the other day about my idea, it was extremely helpful. As I mentioned before, I'm reaching out to several people to gauge interest and a lot of people shared the same feedback that you did, which is exciting!

I really want to build this, but I need to know for sure this is something people like you would be interested in before moving forward. In my experience, a lot of people say they would use or buy something, but only because they're being nice and don't want to hurt someone's feelings. In order for me to know for sure, I need 10 people to pre-order before I move forward with this. If I don't get 10, then I'll simply cancel the pre-order and no one will be charged anything.

Because you were so interested, I'd love to have you become one of the first users. You won't be charged until the product is released, and you'll be one of the first to get access to it. Plus, I'd love for you to be involved in the process of building it, too, just so I can make sure it does what you need it to do.

I'm thinking of selling this in the future for $100 or so, but the pre-order price is currently $50.

If you'd like to be a part of this special group, all you have to do is click on the link below, which will bring you to a page and initiate a checkout process:

[LINK TO PRE-ORDER PAGE]

Thanks again, Jim, and if you have any questions, please don't hesitate to ask!

No matter what method you choose to ask for a pre-order, if you don't get a response within 24 hours send one more follow-up email that checks to make sure the person received it. As I mentioned earlier in the book, the fortune is in the follow-up, so make sure to give them one more message before you dismiss them as not being interested.

Now, to address some common questions related to this particular step:

Q. Is it better to collect pre-orders, or actual payments upfront?

Both pre-orders and actual real-time payments work for validation because both require people to plug in their payment information. The benefit of pre-orders is that there's a higher sense of security because the customer doesn't get charged until the product goes live. The benefit of an actual upfront payment, however, is that you get money in hand that could be used for production and development. If you're bootstrapping and short on cash, collecting a payment upfront could be very helpful, but remember, you owe that person a product or their money back if you don't reach your minimum.

Many people validate by just telling people to send them a certain amount of money directly to their PayPal email address.

Q. How high should you price your product?

There are entire books out there that are dedicated entirely to finding the optimal price for your product. It is an art and a science that I won't get into too much detail about here. What I will say is that you should definitely think ahead of time about how your product will be priced once it's available to the public, and consider offering your early adopters an extremely generous discount. Again, the purpose of this is to validate the business, not make money at this point. That comes later after you validate your product and release it into the wild.

If you're struggling with where to even start, I'd suggest looking at your competitor's prices to get an idea. You have an entire list of products and services in your 3-Ps exercise from way back in Part 3 and this is a great opportunity to use it. Depending on how you feel your product will stack up to the competition, you can price it relative to what's already out there and how you'll compare.

But again, you're just looking to get some kind of payment from prospects to make sure this is something they really want.

Q. What mechanism do you use to collect pre-orders?

There are a number of web solutions available to us to set up a quick page to collect pre-orders. The one I would recommend is Gumroad (**GUMROAD.COM**). Gumroad is a digital good delivery platform, which I use for a number of my products, from my software product, the Smart Podcast Player at **SMARTPOD-CASTPLAYER.COM**, to the eBooks and digital bonuses that come along with the resources on **FOODTRUCKR.COM**. What I like about Gumroad is that it's easy to use, it looks great, and the friction for customers is almost non-existent—meaning there are very few steps required for a customer to complete a purchase, and the flow of the entire process makes sense.

You can start selling before a release date very easily in Gumroad by adding a product and selecting "pre-order" from the options. The release date can be changed at any time, so you can set it to way ahead in the future just to be able to set this up and begin collecting orders.

Even if your idea isn't a digital product, you can still use this system to collect pre-orders. Gumroad accepts credit card payments and PayPal, so it provides an easy way for your audience to say, "Yes, I want this, and I'm willing to pay for it."

Another option is to use services like Celery (**TRYCELERY. COM**), another more robust platform that's made for collecting pre-orders. They also have the option to help you create your own crowdfunding campaign.

Q. How do you keep in contact with your customers after they pay or pre-order?

It's extremely important to keep in consistent contact with your early adopters after they've become a customer. A weekly or bi-weekly broadcast email with progress updates and inquiries for feedback can do the trick. Regular communication will ensure they know what's going on, while also holding you accountable for finishing your product. The worst thing you can do is collect people's money or get their vote of confidence, and then leave them in the dark.

If you don't have an email service provider to collect emails into a list to send broadcast messages to, simply collect all of your customers' email addresses and send them an email all together with their email address in BCC so they are hidden in that message to everyone else.

Another way you can keep people excited is to create a private Facebook group to hold your customers and have them get to know each other, too. This makes it a little easier for you to facilitate discussions, get feedback, and share progress with photos and video updates. You begin to build an environment and culture where raving fans are born, but bear in mind you have to keep people up to date a little more often in a social media environment than you do with email.

Q. What should my minimum be? How many people should I have order before it's a yes?

Does everyone you follow up with need to pay you money in order to green-light your project?

No. Most people will not, even if your solution is perfectly suited for them. Some may not be too keen on paying upfront for something or have the funds to spare at the moment, while others would like to wait until more people are on board with it later in the process.

According to the Diffusion of Innovations theory by Everett Rogers, a professor of communication who published a book in 1962 of the same name, there's a specific progression of adoption of new innovations by users based on a number of factors, including time. The first users (the innovators and early adopters) make up a small percentage of the overall user-base, followed by a surge of new users coming in the early majority and late majority phase, and then the laggards coming in at the end of the cycle.

This adoption curve, seen below, works in our favor and completely parallels what we're doing, because in the beginning we're piloting our idea and fine-tuning it until we eventually scale it up in the early majority phase. Because of this, we can be comfortable knowing that we don't need everyone in our target market to agree to pay upfront in order to understand that it's worth moving forward.

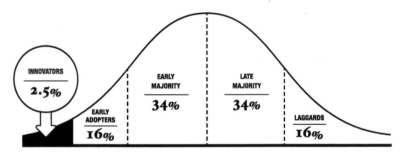

So what's the right number?

Taking into account our research and the interaction we have with our prospects, the goal is to have 10% of those prospects take action with you ahead of the build. That means for every 10 people you pitch here in Step 4, you should try to get at least one person to pre-order or pay. The more interested prospects you speak to, the better, but 10% is a good standard to use here.

So for example, if you talk to 50 prospects, you should try to get at least five to sign up, and that would be a good indication that you have something you should proceed with and build out in full. In terms of how many prospects you should speak to in total, 50 is a good amount. Again, we're validating here so you don't need to talk to the entire world market that's interested in your product—you're just running a small-scale experiment and then can later go full scale with full pricing after you've validated.

This is the fun part! Starting anything new as an entrepreneur is always about working hard up front to see if the work you put in pays off, and it's such a thrill. Be proud that you've made it this far, because many people can only dream of taking action on something like what you're doing. On the flip side, a lot of entrepreneurs will put years into working on something only to finally release it into the wild with little more than a prayer that it will work. You're taking the smarter, more iterative approach toward your first few sales in the validation process.

And when you do get your first order, be sure to celebrate! I remember my first sale in October of 2008. I had to take a walk outside to breathe because I was so excited, and when I got back to my desk another sale notification had popped into my email inbox. Use that momentum moving forward into reaching out to the rest of your prospects, and into your business that you create.

Q. What if I don't get to my minimum?

If you don't reach your minimum, it's not a total loss—not even close. I'm not going to lie to you; it's not going to feel good. But every loss in entrepreneurship can be learned from and used for good later on. And because of the way we've set this up, you can easily hone in on the part that didn't work, figure out why, make changes and then try again.

After a week, if you don't hear back from your prospects

or they reply with a no, you have permission to send them one more email asking why. In *Ask*, Ryan Levesque called this the "Why Do You Hate Me?" email, and it reveals so much about what needs to happen in order for things to work. You don't necessarily have to ask your prospects that exact question because in our particular case during the validation process it's easy to come across as desperate (Ryan puts that question in the final sequence of a series of emails after having close contact with his subscribers for a long period of time). A question of that nature, however, framed a little more honestly can do you a ton of good and reveal quite a bit.

And if you're scared of sending this email, you have to ask yourself that all-important question once again. What's the worst that can happen? You literally have nothing to lose here, but so much to gain, so don't be afraid to hit send.

Here's what that follow-up email might look like:

SUBJECT: *Hey Jim, did I do something wrong?*

Hey Jim, I didn't hear from you after my email to you last week, so I wanted to send you one more. It will only take a second to respond to.

You had previously expressed interest in my product idea but then didn't end up pre-ordering, and I'm emailing to learn why. If you could hit reply and answer this question I'd greatly appreciate it as I'm doing all I can to make sure I create something great for you and others like yourself. Thanks, and I hope to hear from you soon!

As you get replies back, and you likely will, don't take what they say personally. A lot of entrepreneurship is about listening to the feedback from others, and it's not always something you want to hear, but often it's something you have to hear. If someone is disrespectful and rude to you, don't pay any attention to him or her—they have deeper problems going on in their lives and they're taking it out on you. But even respectful and constructive criticisms can be hard to take sometimes.

Entrepreneurship math is weird: One negative comment is greater than 100 positive comments. Just remember every second you stay upset or mad about a negative comment is a second you take away from improving your business, and the lives of others.

I'm confident, however, that at this point you have all the skills you need in order to validate a business idea to continue moving forward with, even if the particular solution you've been testing isn't the one. You've come a long way in this journey, and you're about to graduate to the next stage. There's a reason graduations are called commencement celebrations, and it's because this isn't the end—but of course the very beginning of an entirely new part of life for you.

Before we finish up this book, I know you'd like to see examples of how others have used these validation strategies for their new businesses and products. I've been holding off on examples because these principles and the process are important to understand first, but let's get into specific examples across all different kinds of niches and product ideas. You're likely to find one or two that really speak to you, and you can follow their lead into validating your own solution, too.

18

VALIDATION IN ACTION

n the last chapter, I took you through the four steps of validation. As a reminder, here they are again below for you:

- ► **STEP 1:** Get in front of an audience.

- ► **STEP 2:** Hyper-target.

- ► **STEP 3:** Share your solution.

- ► **STEP 4:** Ask for the transaction.

In this chapter, we're going to see how real life entrepreneurs executed this strategy to validate their business and products ahead of time. In each of the case studies below, which range between all different kinds of businesses across all different markets, you'll get a breakdown of how each person moved forward during each phase of the process. I've also been given special access to emails and some of the tools they used along the way, which are shared within the case studies.

As you go through each of these examples, you'll notice that although they each follow the same basic structure, many of them took the liberty to get creative with how they executed certain steps along the way. You're definitely free to do the same. Here we go!

CASE STUDY #1:
Joey Korenman,
Founder of School of Motion

Joey is the founder and head instructor at School of Motion (**SCHOOLOFMOTION.COM**) where he teaches all things related to motion graphics. Motion graphics is sort of like what I did back in my architecture days with Photoshop, but his stuff actually moves, so he's definitely got some major skills.

He and I connected in early 2015 and I've been hooked on following his progress ever since. He quit his day job to go full-time with School of Motion, and each time he launches a new product he's serving more and more people, and naturally as a result, he's generating more and more income. And to think, it all started with validating an idea before he even built it. Here's how it all happened…

STEP 1: Get in front of an audience.

Joey had built a small following by posting tutorial videos about motion graphics on YouTube and Vimeo, which is where he learned his audience was, because they were all searching for animation tutorials. He attempted to sell software related to animation but soon discovered that the software business did not align with what he liked to do, and he decided from there on out to focus on the education and training aspect of what he was doing. It was at that point he decided he wanted to create and sell a course. Before making the decision to create it entirely, which he estimated would take him a total of three months to complete, he wanted to see if anyone was interested in it first.

STEP 2: Hyper-target.

In his videos, Joey provided a call-to-action to subscribe to his email list. This ensured that everyone who was on his list was interested in learning more about animation, and more importantly, liked the way he taught it. This was key because he would be teaching the six-week training course himself.

STEP 3: Share your solution.

Joey decided to send an email to his entire list. He gave me special access to this early email of his to share with you, which is written below. Make sure to pay attention to how honest Joey is with his prospects, and how he's qualifying himself while building a relationship with them at the same time.

SUBJECT: *Want to get REALLY good at animation?*

I use to suck at animation. Like, really suck at it. No joke.
For the first 6-8 years of my career, anytime I sat down to start a new MoGraph project I had this fear in my stomach. The fear was called "impostor syndrome."
I have absolutely ZERO formal education in Design or Animation.

Kind of silly, considering I am a MOTION DESIGNER, but I imagine there are a lot of MoGraphers like me out there. Maybe you're in this boat.

This fear would manifest whenever I would start animating. I would start moving key frames around, using EasyEase a lot, and hoping that along the way I would "find" some good animation.

I never knew exactly why my animation was good or bad, it was all a gut feeling and throwing darts until one landed.

Imagine my relief when I discovered that, holy crap, there are a bunch of principals out there that can give you a framework to animate around. That this framework has rules you can follow and ways of approaching animation that can make it so much easier to work.

Learning how to animate properly was the key to my success. I'm building a training program to help Motion Graphics artists master Animation.

Learning how to properly animate literally changed my career. It gave me the confidence to open a Motion Graphics shop, act as Creative Director, and supervise teams of animators. It gave me the confidence to teach at the highest level.

This is the program I wish I'd had when I was at the beginning. If this sounds interesting to you, check out the webinar I'm hosting next Wednesday, November 19th.

I'm looking for a small group to be the "beta group" for this course. These first students will get some incredible perks, and will help me make this the best Animation course for MoGraph artists EVER.

Would you like to be one of those students? Click here to learn more.

–JOEY

Notice that, in addition to being completely relatable to his target audience, Joey reveals what his plans are, which is to start a course with a group of early adopters. A webinar is an online seminar, and Joey used it as another validation point to gauge interest because if no one signs up, then he knows this isn't anything anyone wants.

He used GotoWebinar (**GOTOWEBINAR.COM**) to setup the webinar and collect registrants, and he actually had more people register than there were spots available. This showed interest, which is a good start, but again it didn't mean people wanted to necessarily buy what he was about to offer. With 100 people registered, and because of his high price point ($250), he decided that if he could sell 5 spots total upfront, he'd proceed to build out the course.

STEP 4: Ask for the transaction.

On Joey's 45-minute webinar, he started by providing 30 minutes of value by simply giving away a few training techniques that were useful to his audience—a very common and effective strategy on any platform, which accomplished a few favorable things for him:

1. He was able to make sure people got something out of the webinar, whether they ended up becoming a part of his program or not.

2. He was able to build a stronger relationship with his audience because they were hearing his voice and getting to know him and his teaching style even better.

3. He was essentially demonstrating the type of content that would be included in his training course.

Then, for the final 15 minutes, he shared the outline of his animation bootcamp course. He was also very honest that it was not built yet, but that people who signed up as an early adopter would be able to help him make sure it's exactly what they needed along the way.

Here's what Joey included in the outline:

- ► It's a 6-Week Course

- ► Limited number of spots

- ► This class is HARD. It's the P90X of Animation Training.

- ► You'll need 8-10 hours a week to fully immerse in the course.

- ► The more you give, the more you get. Interact.

- ► You must have Adobe CC2014. The course uses After Effects and Flash.

After sharing the call to action to buy, he ended up selling out all 20 spots in 10 minutes and had earned a total of $5,000. A couple of days later, he opened up another 20 spots, sent an email to his list and sold out those additional 20 spots in less than one minute.

Was Joey motivated to build out his course? You're darn right he was! Three weeks later he launched it to his initial users, getting positive and constructive feedback along the way.

His first students also became some of his biggest supporters and were quick to leave glowing testimonials after the course was over. For his second round, he sold out 75 spots at $600 per student, and he keeps earning more and more with each subsequent round. Now, he has a team to help support his growing business.

I'm super proud of what Joey has accomplished, and like I said I've been following his progress super closely after I met him right after his initial launch. I asked him if he could offer a tip for everyone reading this book, and he was more than happy to share one about how he initially felt when he decided to pre-sell his course:

> **"** Mentally, this was a hard thing to leap over. At first, my reactions were 'what a stupid idea,' 'no way people will buy it,' 'you're greedy you're asking for too much money.' But then I had to ask myself, 'why am I afraid of doing this?' And if it didn't work out, I'll just refund people's money, and that's that. At least I gave it a shot and didn't learn that it wasn't going to work after I spent months building the course."

Thanks for being awesome, Joey, and keep rocking those launches and making things move!

CASE STUDY #2:
Bryan Harris, Founder of Video Fruit

I used to subscribe to a few dozens blogs, and probably the same amount of podcasts. I was a content vacuum! The only problem with that is, the more time you spend taking things in, the less time you have to actually get things done. It sucks.

I've since trimmed my subscriptions down to just a select few, and one of the blogs that I read consistently is by Bryan Harris from **VIDEOFRUIT.COM**, who I had the pleasure of interviewing in Session 190 of the SPI Podcast. He always shares amazingly helpful content, and the awesome thing about Bryan is that he has used the validation method to pre-sell several different kinds of products over the years to make sure people want those products first before he builds them. The one I'd like to highlight, however, is his very first product called the *Bootstrapper's Guide to Explainer Videos*. The cool thing is that Bryan started his entire business from scratch inside a small Facebook group in 2013.

Five months later, he quit his job. Here's how he did it…

STEP 1: Get in front of an audience.

Bryan has some serious video making skills—that's one of his superpowers. After getting great feedback on his work he decided to see if he could create a business out of it. He started to build a rapport with the members of a small Facebook group that he knew would be potentially interested in making videos. He began sharing a ton of advice and opening up a lot of his video-making process for free, and in doing so he was allowing people to get to know him and his expertise first, which I love. If there's one thing that will always work for building a strong relationship with an audience quickly, it's providing value first.

STEP 2: Hyper-target.

After a week and several helpful posts later, Bryan shared the following message publicly in the Facebook group:

Last draft of first video using a new method (see post from yday). Final copy out tomorrow. Total hard cost of this video is under $30 with around 2.5 hours of my own time invested.

If you are interested in learning how to make these DM me your email address.

The post also included a short video that people could play to watch to see his work in action. What's cool about this post is that he's not just sharing his progress, but he's also hyper-targeting those in the group who are interested in learning more about his video making methods. Twenty-five people ended up "raising their hands" and sending him a direct message with their email address, and this is when his idea for the *Bootstrapper's Guide to Explainer Videos* course was born.

 Bryan Harris ▸ From Wantrepreneur to Entrepreneur

April 30, 2013 · Nashville, TN

Last draft of first video using a new method (see post from yday). Final copy out tomorrow. Total hard cost of this video is under $30 with around 2.5 hours of my own time invested.

If you are interested in learning how to make these, DM me your email address.

http://www.youtube.com/watch?v=kYbw26ibLeo&feature=youtube_gdata

 App Promo Video (Draft 2)

YOUTUBE.COM

STEP 3: Share your solution.

Next, Bryan then sent the following email to everyone who he had sent him a message:

> *Hey guys,*
> *If you are getting this email you asked me to contact you with some details on how to make the cool promo videos that I posted...*
> *So here's the deal:*
> *Last week I found this really cool way to make awesome videos. I've used it myself over the last week to make several product videos and have even made sales to clients for those videos, all at a very high markup.*
> *I want to make a course showing every detail of how I do it, but I want to pre-sell the course to verify demand...*

I love that Bryan is being super clear and honest about what he wants to do, including the fact that he's going to pre-sell his product to make sure there's a demand.

STEP 4: Ask for the transaction.

Bryan includes a call-to-action in the remaining part of that same email...

> *I have stood up a simple web page here where you can pre-order. The regular cost is $55 but the pre-order price is just $35...*
> *I am offering everyone that gets this email a 25% discount off the already reduced pre-sale price. Just use the offer code "earlybird" at checkout. That will make your total $25.75.*

He set up a quick pre-order page (using **GUMROAD.COM**) and his goal was to get three people out of the 25 (12%) to pre-order the course to show him that there was legitimate interest and people weren't just being nice. Within 48 hours, 19 of the 25 prospects purchased, validating his idea for the course. Yes, this was a massive discount relative to what he was actually offering, but his goal here wasn't to make money, it was to simply validate the idea by having people pay something.

What happened next?

In good form, Bryan kept in constant contact with his customers while building his course between May 2013 and October 2013. He also continued to post regular updates about the course in the same Facebook group, and he started to build an email list. By October, his list grew to 575 people and he was ready to re-launch his course. He re-evaluated the value and pricing structure of his program based on the feedback from his current customers, and when he re-launched his course with a price point of $397, 21 people purchased generating a total of $8,337 in revenue. And by then, his course was already complete.

He also discovered that a lot of people wanted to just pay him to create videos for them, so he took on a number of clients at the same time, many coming from the same Facebook group. It was at that point he was confident enough to make the decision to quit his job and go full-time with his website and services at **VIDEOFRUIT.COM**.

And to think, this all started from just providing value in a small Facebook group. Awesome.

CASE #3: Jennifer Barcelos, Founder of NamaStream.com

The first time I attended a yoga class it nearly broke me—it was difficult! Much more challenging than it looked. But, it was also fun and I couldn't wait to do it again. Lucky for me this class was convenient because I was taking it in my own living room, following instructions from a DVD in the popular P90X home fitness program. I didn't think doing yoga at home like this would work, but it did. As great as it was, it never came across my mind to create a business out of it like Jennifer Barcelos eventually did. Her business, NamaStream (**NAMASTREAM.COM**) enables yoga teachers and entire studios to easily teach yoga lessons to students virtually over the web.

Jennifer was a lawyer and new mom when she decided to participate in a training program called The Foundation (**THEFOUNDATION.IO**), which helped guide her through the process of starting a new software company. Her goal was to create a business that would not only help to support her family, but also fund her non-profit work. With those motivations in mind, she decided to target and conduct market research in the yoga industry because she was a yogi herself for more than 12 years. She knew that her interest in yoga would help her in her research and allow her to relate more easily to those who would eventually become her customers.

Not knowing exactly what kind of business to create at first, she emailed 188 small business owners in the yoga industry to try and get them on the phone to discover what their major pains and problems were. To her surprise, the response rate was actually quite high! Only two of the 188 people she emailed asked her to remove them from her list, and she was able to get on the phone with 74 studio owners and managers and had an idea extraction call with each one.

How was Jennifer able to get such a high response rate?

She offered each person who would get on the phone with her a summary or report of her interviews at the end of the process. This was a genius idea because it made those who she asked to speak to feel more comfortable that this was a serious inquiry, and they knew they would also get something potentially very useful in return. Again, she was very honest when emailing people about what she was doing, and it made people actually want to talk to her more! It became a win for everyone.

Through those phone conversations she actually discovered several ideas she could have built a solution for, but by call number 50 it became apparent that bringing yoga classes online was a major pain and something many studio owners eventually wanted to do, but didn't know how or even where to start.

Before we get into how Jennifer formally validated this idea, let's talk about these phone calls. Obviously, they were an important part of the process in the discovery of what these pains were that studio owners were experiencing, but was Jennifer nervous when dialing in? Absolutely. Here's what she said about how she got over the fear of calling people:

" *I was scared to call, because you get scared of rejection...but everyone I ended up calling said they wanted to talk to me...*

You don't really get over the fear of it until you've done it the first few times. My heart was always racing picking up the phone, but by the end of the conversations, I'd always feel great because of the amazing connections that would happen.

It's funny, because I feel like my brain actually started to associate getting excited with the calls, because they went so well. So I'd actually look forward to them, oddly enough. After I did 10 or 15 calls...there was zero fear."

After Jennifer knew what her target idea was, she then quickly got into the formal validation process.

STEP 1: Get in front of an audience.

Because Jennifer was starting from scratch, her audience became the studio owners and managers that she reached out to individually—first via email, and then on the phone. She could have started by visiting yoga business owner forums and groups online and built relationships with people there, but a direct connection can produce the best information, especially in relation to market research and idea extraction, which was her initial focus.

STEP 2: Hyper-target.

After she discovered the idea she was going to validate, Jennifer reached back out to the people who had expressed that they wanted to somehow put their yoga classes online. Because she already had a relationship with these people, it was very easy to get them back on the phone to discuss this idea even further. Through these follow-up conversations, she was able to have her audience define exactly what it is they wanted.

STEP 3: Share your solution.

After sharing her idea with two people and letting them know that she was going to build this software solution if enough people were interested, one studio owner actually sent her $1,200 via PayPal that day without ever seeing anything! It was then that it became apparent that there was definitely an absolute need here—not just something people said they wanted, but something at least one person wanted to make sure happened, and they paid her to let her know that was the case.

From there, she decided to build out a *wireframe* of the product, a super stripped down version that just shows what something will look and feel like (similar to a prototype), that she would use to visually show people what she was talking about in her future pitches.

STEP 4: Ask for the transaction.

Jennifer reached out to the other business owners who expressed interest and offered a demonstration of the wireframe and what she wanted to build out completely, again, if enough people were interested. She learned even more about what her product should eventually become during those conversations, and in the end she was able to pre-sell her product for $3,600 total before building out the product in full scale.

That was the start, and today **NAMASTREAM.COM** continues to grow as it serves yoga studios around the world by making it incredibly easily to put their classes online, and because Jennifer's pricing model is a recurring monthly or annual payment, she's growing her user base and income streams every single month!

What's great about Jennifer's story is that through the journey of starting her own business and the challenges that came along with it, she learned a lot about herself and what she was capable of. As she explains:

" *I realized that I had been an entrepreneur my whole life. Up until now, I just hadn't owned that truth or been focused on building a business. My decision to own that fact, that title 'I'm an entrepreneur,' has changed every part of me. And it has given me so much confidence and almost a superhero mindset that makes all of my other work even more powerful. I now know that I can figure anything out that I need to learn. It might not be easy, but it's possible.*"

FOR MORE INFORMATION ABOUT JENNIFER AND HER START-UP STORY, CHECK OUT HER INTERVIEW ON THE FOUNDATION BLOG AT HTTP://WWW.THEFOUNDATION.COM/ BLOG/JENNIFER-10-PAYING-CUSTOMERS

CASE #4: Jarrod Robinson, Founder of The PE Geek

When I think of physical education classes three things come to mind:

1. The Presidential Physical Fitness Award

2. Dodgeball, and

3. How upset we all were when the coach announced that we were going to be running a mile, and that it would be timed.

Although I'm sure P.E. coach Jarrod Robinson has commanded his students to go on a few timed mile runs in his past, he's been doing some amazing things in the world of physical education to change how P.E. coaches teach. Combining his passions of P.E. and technology, which he blogs about at **THEPEGEEK.COM**, he has created a number of software solutions and apps to help coaches better keep track of their students' progress and overall fitness. Although he's successful with his software and uses the validation method each time before a new product build, I'd like to rewind to the very first product he validated when he began to monetize. That product was actually an event.

Jarrod started his blog in 2010 on the side while still coaching full-time. It wasn't until 2012, with an email list of zero, that he decided to see if he could turn it into a business. He loved to travel and speak, so he decided to see if he could somehow put on a one-day live workshop to share what he learned with other P.E. teachers. Since then, he's left his full-time job to focus 100% of his efforts on helping other educators, and he's now conducted over a hundred live workshops in cities all over the world!

Here's how he ran through the validation method to make sure it was something worth putting time and money into.

STEP 1: Get in front of an audience.

Jarrod took the longer, slower approach to getting in front of an audience by starting a blog from scratch. Building a following on a platform like a blog, podcast or video channel can take a relatively long period of time, but Jarrod didn't mind doing all of this work simply because he loved it so much, and it was pretty much a side hobby for him in addition to his full-time position. That's probably why he didn't bother to build an email list when he first started—something he admittedly regrets because when he decided he was ready to turn this blog into a business and investigate the possibility of a live-workshop, he wasn't able to send a mass email out to gauge interest, which would have been much easier. So in a sense, he was starting from scratch with this idea.

It was then that Jarrod decided to reach out and get to know a lot of the physical education teachers in and around his home town of Melbourne, Australia. He figured that starting in his hometown would be a great way to quickly run a small-scale experiment with little cost involved. He also figured that if he couldn't convince those he got to know in person to attend, then he would find it hard to believe he could convince people on the other side of the world he didn't personally know to attend, too.

STEP 2: Hyper-target.

One by one, via email, phone and in-person, he reached out to other P.E. teachers in the area and just started to have a conversation with them about technology and physical education to see if they were interested in learning more. He was not yet sharing the idea about his event. Again, he just wanted to make sure this was a topic people were interested in first. If there was no interest, then there was no need to worry about the event at all. Jarrod took note of those who were interested and "raised their hands", and he gathered a small list of interested prospects in the area.

Hyper-targeting one-to-one in real-time like this takes longer, but can be more powerful because you're establishing a more direct relationship right from the start.

STEP 3: Share your solution.

Jarrod later followed up with those who were interested and let them know that he did receive interest from several coaches in the area and was putting on a live, one-day workshop. He gave them a link to a website where they could purchase a ticket for an event that he had already previously scheduled using EventBrite (**EVENTBRITE.COM**). He included a specific date and time, with a location to be announced, and figured that he could easily see if this was something people were interested in based on the number of tickets sold. If there were no tickets sold, then he wouldn't have to worry about putting the workshop together or even finding a venue.

STEP 4: Ask for the transaction.

Jarrod sold the tickets at an early-bird price for an equivalent of $180.00 USD for a six-hour event. Here was the copy that Jared included in the event details:

> *Join world-renowned educator Jarrod Robinson, "The PE Geek," for an action packed one-day workshop focused on emerging technologies to complement teaching and learning in P.E. & Sport Science classes as well as for sports teams. Jarrod will take a look at some of the technologies and emerging pedagogies, which are driving the adoption of learning technologies within the P.E. classroom.*
>
> *In particular attendees will focus specifically on mobile devices such as the iPad and iPod and the capacity these have for transformation within the P.E. classroom. All attendees will be required to bring along a mobile device and will be informed of the necessary apps prior to the workshop commencing.*

Attendees are guaranteed to walk away with best practice actionable ideas for immediate classroom use. Those in attendance will have the opportunity to put their new skills into action with a complete hands-on focus.

BOOK YOUR SPOT NOW TO ENSURE YOU DON'T MISS OUT. AREAS COVERED INCLUDED:

1. *Instant Feedback in the Practical P.E. Classroom*

2. *Video Analysis & Video Based Assessment in the Practical P.E. & Sport Classroom*

3. *Teacher Efficiency and Organization Tools*

4. *Innovative Teacher Resources and Global Collaboration*

5. *Assessment & Portfolios in Physical Education*

6. *Augmented Reality & Flipped Instruction*

7. *& much more*

WHO SHOULD ATTEND?
Any specialist P.E. Teachers or Sports Teacher looking to leverage mobile technologies in their classroom.

Jarrod limited the ticket count to 20 based on the venues he had in mind, and he was just hoping for just few attendees to sign up to validate his concept and get a feel for what the workshop was like.

He sold out all 20 spots.

Since then, he's run these workshops in over 25 countries

around the world. He's also figured out through running multiple events that he can easily get access to venues for these events for free by conducting them in school gyms and giving free access to his workshop to teachers at that school. He's now charging over $300 USD per attendee and has doubled the amount of attendees, which means he's making great money while also helping a lot more people along the way. Better yet, as he's helping physical education teachers, he's also helping their students through them.

The question becomes, however, how does he target cities outside of Melbourne?

Beyond the list he's finally built, Jarrod actually turns to social media to do a lot of his outreach. Here's a simple but effective way Jarrod has been able to use Twitter:

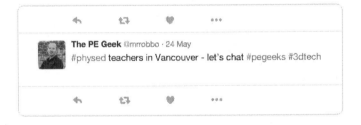

This is simple, however it works. The hashtags being used captures the attention of other P.E. teachers, and if you're a P.E. teacher and you happen to see another one called The PE Geek mention your city, it's easy to respond and say hi. This is how he hyper-targets P.E. teachers in those specific areas.

From there, he eventually talks to these people privately via a direct message or email about the event that he puts on, and sees if there's enough interest in the area before moving forward. He offers a discount code to the event for the first few people to validate it and make it worth the cost of the plane ticket and accommodation. From there, he runs ads on Facebook targeted to teachers in that particular location to fill out the rest of the spots. Again, they are simple, but look like this:

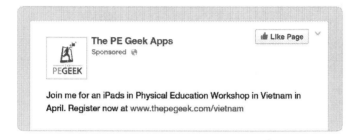

For this single event in Vietnam in April 2015, for example, he was able to sell 30 tickets for a total of $7,873.32 in sales.

Currently, he's in the middle of validating his first big conference with more than 200 attendees in the same manner, reaching out to his contacts (this time via email), and pre-selling tickets beforehand.

The big lesson Jarrod wanted to pass along was this:

" *Although my ticket sales for my events were my true form of validation, I feel that my content was really what started it all. I can't stress how important it is to have amazing content that you give away for free somewhere (in my case, on my blog and podcast) that can then give you opportunities to sell to those who want more of it in different ways. I just happened to choose live events because I wanted to travel and I love to talk and teach directly with people."*

What I love most about Jarrod's case study is that the business model he chose is a direct result of the kind of life he wants to live, and what he enjoys most. He's traveling the world, educating people, and making money all at the same time!

CASE STUDY #5: Noah Kagan, Founder of SumoJerky.com

I love beef jerky. It's delicious, it's healthy, and it makes me feel like I could survive in the wild (although that's probably not true). What's also cool about jerky is that Noah Kagan was able to pre-sell and validate a monthly beef jerky subscription service called Sumo Jerky (**SUMOJERKY.COM**) in only 24 hours. Today it has thousands of monthly subscribers.

Noah runs another company called App Sumo (**APPSUMO.COM**) and this jerky business actually came as a result of a challenge on that site. He challenged himself to make a $1,000 profit in less than 24 hours and let his community come up with the idea. Noah could pick from any of the ideas that were proposed, but he wasn't allowed to use any of his available networks on AppSumo or his blog to promote it. Beef jerky was one of the options, and because he loved trying new and delicious jerky, it was the obvious choice for him.

It ended up doing so well that in order for the company to keep growing, he had to eventually hand it off to another person because AppSumo was still his main gig. Ryan Luedecke is now considered "Chief Jerk" at Sumo Jerky, but below I'll share how Noah got it all started.

The validation process can sometimes take days or even weeks because it takes time to talk to the right people and get in front of the right audience, and because it's an iterative process you can make sure things are green-lit before moving on to the next step.

Because Noah is insane and gave himself only 24 hours to make $1,000 in profit, he combined a lot of the validation method steps into one to be able to meet his deadline. So as opposed to the cases we've already covered, the validation steps are all swirled together (see if you can spot them). With that said, you'll see how he followed the same journey and was able to meet his goal.

A business centered on beef jerky could be anything, but to refine his idea, he began to talk to people and ask questions about their beef jerky eating habits. Here is a list of questions he came up with to help him figure out what people might want:

1. How often do you eat jerky?

2. Where and how do you decide to buy your jerky?

3. What would make you pay for jerky right now?

4. What's your hesitation in not buying right now?

Through conversations with friends and random people, he discovered that those who ate jerky usually didn't think too much about the jerky they buy, they just like it because it's healthy and they're open to trying all different types. When I think about my own jerky-buying habits, it falls perfectly in line with Noah's findings. I don't think at all about the brand choice or even the flavor, I'm usually more inclined to get something if it's convenient, like at Target or if I happen to see some at a gas station when I'm hungry during a road trip.

Noah's focus was going to be selling jerky as a healthy and convenient snack. He decided to target young professionals who already ate healthily, and also offices, which is smart because many of them buy snacks for their employees in bulk already. A subscription service made perfect sense for these types of prospects, but again he had to validate it to make sure.

Because part of the rules of the challenge was that he couldn't use his existing business networks or email lists, he simply started by reaching out to offices in the local area. He also reached out to friends and people he thought would like it, just to see if it was something they were interested in. Furthermore, he was also able to reach new people by asking his friends for referrals, which later became a huge part of his overall strategy and helped him gain a lot more exposure rather quickly.

Here's an email that he sent to one of his friends:

> Zack,
>
> I'm testing out a new venture, figured you'd like it:
> **Monthly jerky service.**
>
> $40 / month is enough for healthy jerky every single day. About $1.42/day for delicious snackage. Trying to sell blocks of 3 ($120) or 6 ($240) months.
>
> you in?
>
> limiting to 20ish people today so I can place a bulk order for next week
>
> **[HIS PAYPAL EMAIL WENT HERE]**
> XOXO
>
> **–NOAH**
> p.s. know any offices that buy snacks I should chat it up with???

What impressed me most about Noah was not just the fact that he was quick to act (although having the deadline in place and an audience watching his every move probably helped with that), but that he knew exactly how many beef jerky subscriptions he needed to sell to profit $1,000.

Unlike digital products like software and eBooks, which have an initial production cost but can then be distributed without having to replenish inventory, physical goods and consumables require a lot more thinking when it comes to the budget and feasibility of the business.

If you're getting into a physical goods type of business, it's important that you check the economic viability of the business. How much will it cost to produce the item? How much will it cost to ship the product? What do you think it will sell for, and how much profit margin will you be left with? Although you're still validating your idea, it's good to know what these numbers are to discover any red flags. You may not be under the gun like Noah, and you may not have a crazy goal like earning $1,000 profit within the first day, but understanding the basic numbers can help you determine pricing strategies and where you could potentially save money down the road.

Noah didn't make beef jerky himself, so he planned to get it from suppliers. After calling jerky suppliers in the nearby area and determining the cost of goods and any discounts he could get for bulk orders, he created a budget to see how many monthly subscriptions he would need to sell, and at what price point, to meet his $1,000 goal.

Revenue	
	Planned
Per Sale	20
Cost	
Jerky	10
Shipping	1.5
Profit / sale	8.5
#sold	132
Revenue	$2,640.00
Costs	$1,518.00
Paypal fees (boo)	$118.00
Profit	$1,003.20
Margins	38.00%

You'll notice that his sales price is $20 in his budget, while in his initial email to Zack he was offering the service for $40/month. This was on purpose because he wanted to see just how much money people were willing to pay for this service, because he really had no idea what people would pay. He overshot, knowing it would be easier to lower the price to please people, than raise it later.

Also, because he was selling a subscription service, he knew that selling 3-month or 6-month plans is where he would gain the most ground, as opposed to selling 1-month plans. This was tough to do, considering it wasn't even a business that existed yet, but he was determined and kept reaching out to more people.

After nine more hours of calling, especially with those who

his friends referred, he hit his goal. Noah earned $3,030 in total revenue, which left him with $1,135 profit! This was no easy feat, however, and Noah even said himself that he hadn't worked that hard in a long time. So why did he do it? Two reasons: first, to show that it's possible, even in a niche he didn't know he was going to get into a day earlier, and second, to show that it's not easy. It takes work, but Noah took away a lot of lessons he passed on to his audience after the experiment ended. I've listed his takeaways below, because they are massively important:

1. **Real-time communication (Skype, Gtalk, texting, phone-calls) wins.** This was the most effective way in selling vs. more passive forms (emails, Facebook/ Twitter posts).

2. **Ask for referrals.** If someone isn't interested, ask who is. If someone is interested, just ask for one person who they think will like it too. I incentivized this with an extra month of jerky with any successful referral.

3. **Downsells work.** If someone didn't want 3 months, I asked if they were okay with just 1 month of jerky.

4. **You can't sell everyone.** With limited time, anyone who did not eat jerky or didn't care about high-quality specialty jerky wasn't worth selling to.

5. **Focus on what already works.** Quickly, I noticed offices already order snacks AND have larger budgets to expense things (perfect).

6. **Ask people what they want.** If people liked a certain type of jerky already, I noted that and will just get them

the kinds they like. Why guess? Work backwards from what people already want.

7. **Social media is noisy.** I posted twice on both Facebook/ Twitter to make sure anybody who knows me has a better chance of finding my jerky. I usually assume one tweet should reach everyone, it doesn't.

8. **You don't need to spend a lot of money to start a business.** With only 24 hours and $7.99, I got this biz going. You don't need to spend tons of money and time to validate a business.

9. **The secret to success…is work.** That's it. It's hard and tiring but if you want it, you can do anything.

10. **You've got to ask. I focused on people who I thought the jerky would genuinely be good for.** It is a bit uncomfortable but I noticed that's generally the case when you aren't promoting something you believe in.

11. **Build (or maintain) your network.** If you complain you don't have enough people to sell to, build it now. I noticed I hadn't reached out to many friends in awhile. You have to tend to your "garden" or it will decay.

What it all boils down to is **you**. If you really want it and are willing to work, the lifestyle you want is available to you.

I recently asked Noah what he would say to someone who is starting from absolute zero, no friends on social media or anything like that, and here's what he said:

" *I'd recommend people joining groups where their target audience and prospects live and getting involved. It's not difficult; it just takes work. That's where you start.*"

IF YOU'D LIKE TO LEARN MORE ABOUT THE START OF SUMO JERKY, YOU CAN READ MORE ABOUT IT ON THE APP SUMO BLOG AT HTTP://WWW.APPSUMO.COM/SUMO-JERKY.

ADDITIONALLY, YOU CAN FIND AN EXCLUSIVE VIDEO INTERVIEW WITH NOAH KAGAN IN CHAPTER 18: VALIDATION IN ACTION OF THE WILL IT FLY COMPANION COURSE, WHERE HE REVEALS MORE BEHIND THE SCENES INFO ABOUT SUMO JERKY. HE ALSO SHARES HOW HE WOULD VALIDATE A MATTRESS BUSINESS, WHICH ACTUALLY MADE ME AND MY FILM CREW WANT TO TRY IT OUT, JUST TO SEE IF IT WOULD WORK.

CASE STUDY #6: You!

The next case study I'd like to share might be yours! In future editions of *Will It Fly?*, I'll not only include more updated strategies for business and product validation, but I'll also be including more case studies from people like you! All you have to do is send me an email at **PAT@WILLITFLYBOOK.COM** with the subject line **I'M FLYING** and a quick description of what business you validated and how you did it!

I'll be able to keep track of the incoming success stories and I'll reach out to you to get more information if I choose to highlight your story. It doesn't matter what niche you get into or how big or small you validate. Share it, and I'd love to hear it!

And a special thanks to everyone who let me feature their case study in this edition!

In the Companion Course (**WILLITFLYBOOK.COM/COURSE**) I'll be adding more validation case studies for you to check out, including exclusive audio and video interviews that get deep into the strategies that new business owners used to get started.

If you reached this part of the book, I wish I could tell you in person how awesome you are. Seriously. Whether you followed the steps along the way to validate your own idea, or you took a first pass at reading all the way through so you knew what was coming first, I want to thank you.

We've done a lot together. In the beginning pages of this book, we put your idea aside for a bit and looked inward at what you want in life, and what makes you, you. That's not always an easy thing to do, and I'm thankful you opened up during the process. I hope in my opening up to you I made it a little easier for you to run through those exercises for yourself.

Then, we learned how to mind map and define what our ideas actually were, and we even got over the fear of talking to others about it. Truth be told, I still get nervous when I have to talk to others about my ideas. I don't think the fear ever goes away, we simply learn how to control it and use it to our advantage.

After that, you created your Market Map and also your Customer P.L.A.N. to get a full understanding of the target market you were entering, and the customers that you will serve. Both the Market Map and Customer P.L.A.N. will become useful tools for you as you move forward and grow your business. And then of course, you came up with your own "elixirs" to cure the pains of your customer, and we went through the validation method to put at least one of those solutions to the test.

Now, as we approach the final chapter of this book, I imagine you walking into an aircraft hangar with your flight helmet in one of your hands, moving in slow motion like they do in the movies. In the background, I hear music that's slowly building and increasing tempo as you approach your fighter plane and get ready for battle.

I want to tell you that no matter where you are with your idea right now, even if your idea didn't "pass the test" the first time around, you are made for entrepreneurship. In addition to writing this book to validate ideas, I wrote it to validate you as an entrepreneur, someone who knows that win or fail, each step you take is one step closer to success. The only true failure is giving up. It takes hard work and patience to succeed, and I know that you know that because you're here reading these words after all we've done together.

There will likely be a number of people who don't get this far into the book, and that's okay. They'll probably leave 1-star reviews on Amazon and complain about how much work it takes, that the exercises are dumb or that these validation strategies don't work at all. If that happens and you see it, let it be. Don't reply. Don't respond. Don't get upset. There are people in this world that need you, and they are the ones that deserve your time and attention, so focus on serving them, and you will be rewarded down the road.

I have one more chapter for you before we finish up. It's not long, but it's everything I need to share with you before we close. It's truly been a pleasure to be a part of this journey with you. Let's finish strong.

PART 5

ALL
SYSTEMS
GO

" **The secret of flight is this—
you have to do it immediately,
before your body realizes it is
defying the laws.**"

—MICHAEL CUNNINGHAM

19

COUNTDOWN

'm proud of you.

You took actions and made conscious decisions like a boss. You learned more about your target market than they even know about themselves. You stepped out of your comfort zone and put yourself out there without knowing what would happen, but wanting to find out. And now, you have direction and confidence to go along with that, too.

You're ready. All systems go.

SO WHERE DO YOU GO FROM HERE?
WHAT'S NEXT?

The worst thing you could do is stop. You've got momentum on your side so definitely take advantage of that, which means knowing what to do next and then taking action to make it happen. But you already know that, and likely already know what's next.

You've served a small sample of your target market, and the rest of it is now waiting for you. It's time to go full scale, but at the same time remember that it's about taking one step at a time. Keep in mind the iterative process we used throughout this book to get to this point, and keep an open mind that things are not always going to go according to plan, but with the right guidance, you will make it work.

Before launching anything into space, NASA displays a countdown clock that shows how much time is left until liftoff. During the countdown, there's a specific sequence of events that happen, which includes a final check on the system to ensure that everything is ready for launch. During our final pages here in this book, I wanted to share five final thoughts to take with you as you graduate into the next level of entrepreneurship.

5.

BREAK IT DOWN AND APPRECIATE THE SMALL WINS ALONG THE WAY.

Building a successful business is no easy task, nor is it a small one. It's easy to feel the weight of the work you put upon yourself and because people like you and me are so ambitious, we have big visions and create huge goals for ourselves. That's great, but sometimes we lose sight of the light at the end of the tunnel and we lose our way.

I know, because that's how I felt when I started writing this book. This was a huge project for me, not because it was an ambitious topic to begin with (it was), but because I wanted it to be the best resource available on the topic and worth every minute of your time. I made it so big in my head that I was hardly able to get anything done at first. After four weeks of two- or three-hour writing sessions every morning, I literally had an outline and about 2,000 words to show for it, which calculates to about six or seven pages of work. At that rate, it would have taken me two years to finish this book!

It was like that until I finally got some much needed advice from my good friend, Azul Terronez, who helped hold me accountable during the book writing process. Just knowing he was there checking on me helped, but it was when he told me to break down the book into little chunks that I started to finally make progress.

In my head, the book transformed itself into a series of blog posts, which became a lot easier to manage and a lot less intimidating. When going into a writing session, instead of having only completed another 1% of the book, I was able to complete 100% of one chapter. In the end it's the same amount, but when you're in the middle of a big project a small win can mean the difference between feeling miserable about the work you've done or feeling great about it. And of course when you feel great about something, you want to keep going.

One thing I've learned as an entrepreneur is to celebrate the small wins along the way. (The same rule applies to writing books.) After you break down your big goals into manageable chunks, be proud of yourself for getting to each new milestone. As an entrepreneur, you have to do that or else you'd drive yourself crazy.

It's like when you're raising a baby and you celebrate every little milestone along the way—the first smile, the first laugh, the first roll over, the first coo, the first full night's sleep, the first crawl, the first words, the first time eating solid food, and the first steps. As parents, we *need* to celebrate these small wins because they become the happy moments amongst the overwhelming nature of what it takes to raise a child. I think this is why my wife, April, and I always tell each other every little new thing the kids seem to learn and pick up along the way.

As you move forward with your business, be sure to think big, but break those big goals down into little bite-sized milestones, and celebrate your work as you conquer them.

4.

GET SUPPORT.

Behind every successful entrepreneur are people who support what they do and add value to their lives.

Now, this doesn't necessarily mean you have to build a team—at least not right out of the gate. It took me four years to finally hire someone to help me manage parts of my business, but honestly I wish I had done it sooner.

Since I started my business back in 2008, I've always had some kind of support system and people to talk to, and that support has been vital to my success. After I was let go from my architectural position support came first from my then-fiancée, April, who gave me the courage to enter the world of entrepreneurship and believe in myself.

Support from loved ones is extremely helpful, but I also know that it's not always possible, especially when you're just starting out. A common email I receive comes from those who have a hard time trying to convince their significant other that the work they are doing to start a business is worth it. My advice would be to stop trying to convince them, but rather just have an honest conversation about what you're doing, and why. The why is important because if they can see you're coming from a place of support and wanting to make things better, then typically they'll begin to at least understand. In some cases, however, it's going to take more than a conversation. If you find yourself in that situation, I would avoid talking about business because it just stirs things up. Instead, work to get small, tangible meaningful wins that you can share.

Whether you have support from loved ones or not, there is support out there for you elsewhere. I'm a big fan of connecting with other like-minded people who all help support each other in reaching their goal. As Jim Rohn once said, "You are the average of the five people you spend the most time with." So I make sure to surround myself with as many smart, ambitious, and kind people as possible.

I have business-related friends who I connect with from time to time, and those conversations alone play a big role in what I learn and what decisions I make in my business, but more than that, I formally connect with various groups of people on a consistent basis to learn even more and be held accountable. I help the other members of my group, and in return they help me. It's like a modern-day Knights of the Round table, where no one person is the leader of the group but they are all there to help each other for a greater good. These types of structured groups are called mastermind groups; a term coined by Napoleon Hill in his book *Think and Grow Rich*.

I highly recommend you connect with other entrepreneurs in a formal, consistent manner like in a mastermind group. It's a topic I've spoken about before, so if you're interested in learning more just head to the following URL:

HTTP://WWW.SMARTPASSIVEINCOME.COM/HOW-TO-BUILD-A-WINNING-MASTERMIND-GROUP/

3.

TREAT YOUR CUSTOMERS LIKE GOLD.

Your customers, your followers, your subscribers, readers, viewers, and listeners—these people are the lifeblood of your business, and you must treat them like gold.

As you start to focus on building and growth, it's very easy to lose sight of the fact that there are actual people on the other end of those numbers. When you realize that your subscribers are people, and your traffic is people and your social media following is people, you begin to treat them in a way they want to be treated. Nobody wants to be treated like a number.

When you're just starting out, being small is your advantage. You get to research the market a little easier and get a bird's-eye perspective on things like we did back when you created your Market Map. You also have the opportunity to more easily interact with your target customer and create real connections. These are ties much better and stronger than the big guys in the space who are so busy they don't have the time of day to even answer an email.

Beyond that, always be looking out for your target customer. What's in it for them? What will best serve them? As a reminder, your earnings are a byproduct of how well you serve your audience, so even though we've already done a lot of research about who they are, over time you're going to have the opportunity to connect with them, learn more about them, and serve them even better. Never let those opportunities slip by you.

Lastly, create special moments for your customers. Unexpected surprises. It's easy for you to get into a rhythm of doing the same thing over and over again to serve your audience. Don't let your interactions become routine. Surprise them every now and then with something memorable.

Never forget to treat your customers like gold.

2.

REMEMBER WHY.

You've gone through this entire process, picked up and read the pages of this book, for what?

I can't answer that question for you, only you can, and you must.

Q. Why have you decided to become an entrepreneur?

We worked together to uncover your why in Mission Design way back in the beginning of this book. Can you recall everything you wrote down in the four sectors during the airport exercise?

To show you just how important it is to continually be reminded of our whys, find the paper airplane that you folded back in the first exercise and open it up. I'll bet that you forgot that you had written all of those things. You probably remember some of those items, but already just during the time you've worked through this book, you forgot some of those things. Just imagine how much more you may forget as you go deeper into entrepreneurship, working harder than ever and with even more on your mind.

It's important to know what to do, but it's even more important to remember why you do what you do. Keep your paper airplane close by as a reminder of what all of this is about for you.

1.

ENJOY THE RIDE.

And finally, although the entrepreneurial journey can be filled with many challenges and failures, make sure you enjoy the ride, too. This path has chosen you as much as you have chosen it.

Lift off.

SO WHERE DO YOU GO FROM HERE?

Well, my website and podcast at SMARTPASSIVEINCOME.COM were created to help budding entrepreneurs like you! That's where I share how to build your business from the ground up through the experiments that I run in my own businesses—both old and new. All of the information on the website is free, so if you'd like to check it out, visit SMARTPASSIVEINCOME.COM/LIFTOFF so I know you're coming from this book. I look forward to serving you there!

Cheers, and here's to you and your success! If you'd like to let me know what you thought of this book, shoot a message to me on Twitter at @PatFlynn and make sure to use the hashtag #WillItFly. Thanks again!

THE WILL IT FLY COMPANION COURSE
(FOR FREE!)

Several chapters in this book include thought experiments and exercises to help you find and validate a business idea that works for you. To get the most out of this book, some of these exercises will require you to write a few things down and organize them in a specific manner.

Although it's not required, I highly recommend you access the free *Companion Course* that I've created for you at the following website:

WILLITFLYBOOK.COM/COURSE

In this free course, you'll get access to supplemental materials including printable worksheets, PDF files, video instructions, and a list of resources mentioned in the book. The materials in this course are organized by the sections and chapters of this part of the book, which makes it easy for you to find what you need as you read along.

There's also an additional bonus section with content beyond what is shared here in the book, including additional case studies and interviews. I'll be adding more material in this bonus section over time, so make sure to visit the web address and get free access to it now. Thanks, and I'll see you on the inside!

Visit the following link to get free access to your *Will It Fly?* bonus materials now:

WILLITFLYBOOK.COM/COURSE

RESOURCES FOR STARTING YOUR BUSINESS

Ideas are meant to be acted on, and I sincerely hope you are inspired to start a business. On my website, Smart Passive Income, I have assembled a comprehensive list of the tools, services, and products (both free and paid) that will help you run your business effectively and efficiently.

SMARTPASSIVEINCOME.COM/RESOURCES

What follows is an abbreviated list of the tools and services that will help you in the first stages of forming your online business. I am often able to offer exclusive discounts or extra features to my readers—to take advantage of those deals, go to:

SMARTPASSIVEINCOME.COM/RESOURCES.

SETTING UP YOUR BUSINESS

BLUEHOST: WEBSITE HOSTING AND DOMAIN PURCHASING
Ninety-nine percent of my websites are hosted on Bluehost. They make the initial setup a breeze with their one-click Word-Press installation. Best of all, their customer service, via phone or chat, is excellent—patient and knowledgeable. I highly recommend using Bluehost for your first site and beyond! (I have negotiated special pricing for my readers; check out the link at **SMARTPASSIVEINCOME.COM/**resources before purchasing.)

BLUEHOST.COM

LEGALZOOM: ONLINE BUSINESS FORMATION (INCORPORATION, LLCS, AND DBAS)

In order to protect your personal assets, I highly recommend that you make your business a separate legal entity. Whether that's an LLC, a corporation, or a non-profit, LegalZoom can assist you with the paperwork. I have used LegalZoom for business formation and found it clear and easy to use. They are not a law firm (and neither am I), but they can help you connect with a lawyer in your state if you need additional assistance.

LEGALZOOM.COM

CONVERTKIT / AWEBER: EMAIL MARKETING PLATFORMS

The biggest mistake I made early in my business was waiting to start an email list. Your email list is the very center of your online business—your method of connecting directly with your audience. I use and recommend both ConvertKit and AWeber. They offer slightly different features; take some time to choose the platform that is right for you.

CONVERTKIT.COM / AWEBER.COM

GOOGLE APPS FOR WORK: EMAIL ADDRESSES AND FILE SHARING FOR YOUR DOMAIN

One of the ways to show others your business is serious is through your email address by have an address at **YOURDOMAIN.COM** (such as **PAT@SMARTPASSIVEINCOME.COM**). In addition to email, Google Apps for Work gives you custom storage using Google Drive.

APPS.GOOGLE.COM

ORGANIZING YOUR CONTENT & TASKS

CoSchedule: Editorial calendar management for WordPress

This tool has two main benefits: scheduling and collaboration. It helps you build an entire marketing campaign around your blog posts, so that when you post a blog post, you also kick off a series of posts to social media. The tool is built for collaboration, so that you can schedule individual tasks for each member of your team.

COSCHEDULE.COM

Trello: Project and task management

Trello is an excellent tool for managing projects visually. Use it to organize a lot of information and stay on track. While it is an excellent tool for working with large teams, it's also great for solo projects. It's great for managing product/project launches or planning editorial content. Trello is a freemium tool (free, with paid premium accounts).

TRELLO.COM

Slack: Team-based communication

If you have a team, Slack is the best way to communicate. It's a messaging platform that archives your communication, allowing you to talk to your team without using email. You can share files, have group discussions, and send private messages real-time. It has made communication with my team streamlined and productive while retaining the fun sense of humor within our team. Slack is a freemium tool.

SLACK.COM

Calendly: Online appointment scheduling

Scheduling time with people is a pain. Calendly helps you reduce the back-and-forth emails. You configure your available time slots; with one link the other person can schedule himself or herself on to your calendar. Calendly is a freemium tool.

CALENDLY.COM

OPTIMIZING YOUR WEBSITE

LeadPages: Landing pages and opt-in forms

The best tool, hands down, for easily creating high-quality landing and squeeze pages, including webinar registration forms, thank-you pages, and more. It's a staple in most people's toolbox. I am also an advisor for this company, and I couldn't have grown my email list to over 100,000 as fast without them.

LEADPAGES.NET

SumoMe: Website and email list optimization

How well is your website performing? When visitors arrive, do they sign up for your email list? SumoMe is filled with tools to help you grow your website and your email list. There are tools to capture email addresses, increase social sharing, understand your site analytics, and more. It integrates with all the major email providers. Try out one tool or use them all. SumoMe is a freemium tool.

SUMOME.COM

SETTING UP A PAID COURSE

Teachable: Course building platform

If your big idea is to create an online course, then Teachable is for you. It's an easy-to-use platform for building and selling online courses. The courses look great, no coding work necessary. Go to **WILLITFLYBOOK.COM/COURSE** to see a course built on Teachable. Teachable is a freemium tool.

TEACHABLE.COM

SETTING UP YOUR PODCAST

Pat's Step-by-Step How to Start a Podcast Tutorial: Podcast setup advice

My six-video, free step-by-step tutorial that will help you get your podcast up and running as soon as possible! I walk you through recording, editing, and iTunes submission.

PODCASTINGTUTORIAL.COM

Skype with Ecamm Call Recorder or Pamela: Software for recording interviews

The best method I've found for recording podcasts is quite simple: use Skype plus a recording plugin. For Mac computers, use Ecamm Call Recorder; for PCs, use Pamela for Skype.

SKYPE.COM

ECAMM.COM/MAC/CALLRECORDER/

WWW.PAMELA.BIZ/

Smart Podcast Player: Podcast player for WordPress websites

Many of your podcast listeners will choose to listen directly from your website, but most web-based podcast players are dumb. Not this one! This is a solution I built for myself that I'm happy to share with the world, and so far the response has been amazing! It looks pretty, has social sharing, and will keep listeners on your site longer.

SMARTPODCASTPLAYER.COM

BUSINESS BOOKS

These are the books I recommended throughout *Will It Fly?*.

- ► *The 4-Hour Workweek: Escape 9-5, Live Anywhere, and Join the New Rich* –TIMOTHY FERRISS

- ► *Ask. The Counterintuitive Online Formula to Discover Exactly What Your Customers Want to Buy...Create a Mass of Raving Fans...and Take Any Business to the Next Level* –RYAN LEVESQUE

- ► *Crush It!: Why NOW Is the Time to Cash In on Your Passion* –GARY VAYNERCHUK

- ► *Essentialism: The Disciplined Pursuit of Less* –GREG MCKEOWN

- ► *The ONE Thing* –GARY KELLER AND JAY PAPASAN

► *Virtual Freedom: How to Work with Virtual Staff to Buy More Time, Become More Productive, and Build Your Dream Business* –CHRIS DUCKER

LET GO:

MY UNEXPECTED PATH FROM PANIC TO PROFITS AND PURPOSE

–Pat Flynn

Let Go is Pat Flynn's touching memoir about overcoming adversity through a commitment to pursuing your own path. When a job layoff in a bad economy forced Pat to reconsider his career as an architect, he found an unexpected path forward. Along the way, Pat managed to not only achieve financial success, but more importantly discovered what matters most: passion and purpose.

In *Let Go*, Pat reveals the inside story of his transformation into one of today's most beloved thought leaders in the areas of Internet business, online marketing, and lifestyle entrepreneurialism. He shares the challenges and feelings he faced as he pieced together what has become a thriving online enterprise.

If you share Pat's impulse to pursue your own path, then you'll enjoy reading *Let Go*. After all, we all must confront the same risky idea if we are to unlock our true potential: letting go.

You can get free access to the audio version of *Let Go* in the bonus section of the *Will It Fly* Companion Course, or get access to the text version at this link:

WILLITFLYBOOK.COM.COM/LETGO

ACKNOWLEDGEMENTS

Thank you, first and foremost, to the fans of SMARTPASSIVEINCOME.COM—the readers, listeners, and viewers who have not only motivated and supported me throughout the years, but have kept me honest and on the right path. I've seen what success has done to some people, including some very close friends who I cannot call my friends anymore. I'm lucky to have an audience that is not afraid to speak up, be honest, and help keep me away from the dark side, and for that I am truly thankful. I will continue to serve you through the work that I do.

I'd also like to give a huge shout out to Team Flynn: Matt Gartland, Mindy Holahan, Jessica Lindgren, Janna Maron, Dustin Tevis, Caleb Wojcik, Bryan Dwyer, and everyone else who has played a role in the SPI journey. They are all superheroes to me in their own special way. Their talents are impressive and unmatched, but what means the most to me is their alignment with my value and desire to serve my audience and make the Internet a better place. As this engine continues to grow, they are always finding ways to keep it well oiled and running smoothly. I look forward to everything else we build together!

Another important group of people that I'd like to thank are those who are in my mastermind groups with me: Jaime Tardy, Todd Tresidder, Josh Shipp, Roderick Russell, Cliff Ravenscraft, Michael Stelzner, Ray Edwards, Mark Mason, and Leslie Samuel. These amazing individuals know my business and me more than anyone, and have directly contributed to helping me reach several important milestones in my journey, including the publishing of this book. I'm very lucky to have had their encouragement, accountability and brutal honesty along the way to make sure I do what I set out to do, and continue to believe in myself when that "resistance" in my head tries to stop me in my tracks.

I'd also like to thank Azul Terronez—without him this book would have never been published. Originally a student of mine, he became an amazing teacher who coached and guided me throughout the entire process of writing this book. Ever since we sat in a Barnes and Noble to brainstorm book topics together, I was met with a lot of self-resistance during this journey, and he was always there to bail me out. I hope everyone who struggles with a goal has a friend like Azul to hold them accountable and keep them moving forward.

And I can't, of course, forget my brother from another mother, Chris Ducker. Even though he's running multiple businesses from the other side of the world, we manage to have weekly conversations that range from tear-inducing hilarity about nothing, to extremely serious matters that could change the course of our businesses and lives. I'm truly blessed to have a friend like Chris who not only cares about me, but my family, too— even though he did pelt a water balloon point blank at my wife's face once. We'll argue about pronunciations of words like "niche" and "chamomile" until forever, but we have each other's backs no matter what. It's hard to find a friend like that, and I'm thankful I have one in Chris.

I'd also like to thank several unofficial mentors who have inspired me in some way leading up to this point. Jeremy Frandsen and Jason Van Orden who in 2008 helped me realize that working for myself was possible and gave me the advice I needed when starting out. Tim Ferriss, whose book *The 4-Hour Work Week* inspired me to build businesses in a way that work for us, instead of the other way around. To Gary Vaynerchuk for showing me what it means to be authentic, and how refreshing that is. To Michael Hyatt, for not only helping me realize what's possible when a great team is behind you, but also being a role model related to family and business. To Ramit Sethi, for helping me understand that it was important to become the CEO of my own work. Chalene Johnson, for her generosity and what it really means to have raving fans.

Hal Elrod has also played a special role in my journey. His book, *The Miracle Morning*, radically changed my life and productivity, and beyond the journaling and meditation I do every day now, as a result of his teachings, I was also able to make time for myself in the morning to get this book done. Between 6:00 a.m. until whenever my kids woke up was my time to write, and I'm so appreciative of the fact that I now realize just how important my morning routine is. And this, coming from someone who once swore to only getting work done at night and never being able to become a morning person ever. I stand corrected, and Hal, thank you for the help you've given me, and I'm thankful to call you my friend.

To everyone who agreed to help promote and share this book in some way, shape, or form, especially those who allowed me to guest post on their blogs or be a guest on their podcast leading up to the launch of *Will It Fly*. You definitely helped give it the wind it needed to reach incredible heights, and although there are too many of you to thank, you know who you are and I hope you realize just how thankful I am for your support.

A special shout out must also be made to Jay Papasan, co-author of *The ONE Thing*. That book played a critical role in helping me focus as I continued to work through this book, which was my One Thing for six months leading up to the launch, and for that I thank both Jay and his co-author, Gary Kellar. Jay was very helpful in allowing me to pick his brain a bit as I wrote the book, especially related to the Airport Test and History Test in Part 1.

And of course, I wouldn't be where I'm at today without my wife, April, who is the most underrated member of Team Flynn. She does so much to support the work that I do, not only in her words of encouragement but also in her actions as an amazing stay-at-home mother. She works harder than I do, sacrifices so much to dedicate 100% of her time to the kids and being a mom, and does this all without fans, followers, fame, or worldly praise. For Keoni and Kailani (our two kids) if you read this in the future, which I'm sure you will, I hope you realize that this book, and everything that I've been able to build over time, has always been and will be a team effort between your mom and me.

To all who read this, here's to you and your future, and making It fly.

ABOUT SMART PASSIVE INCOME (SPI)

Smart Passive Income (**WWW.SMARTPASSIVEINCOME.COM**) is a resource run by Pat Flynn that teaches individuals how to start and run a successful online business. The site includes step-by-step advice for building, launching, and growing an online business through passive income. SPI is dedicated to providing ethical business advice that has been properly tested.

Smart Passive Income includes a variety of free resources to assist you:

THE SPI BLOG contains detailed, step-by-step advice and strategies for each stage of your business, as well as in-depth reviews of tools and resources.

THE SMART PASSIVE INCOME PODCAST is a weekly, top-ranked podcast with expert interviews and reader success stories (available in iTunes).

THE ASK PAT PODCAST is a daily, bite-sized podcast where Pat answers questions from listeners about their businesses (available in iTunes).

SPI TV is a video podcast with book recommendations, keynote replays, and step-by-step software tutorials designed to provide inspiration and support to business owners (available in iTunes and on YouTube).

Thanks for reading this book! By now you've done a lot of hard work testing and refining your business idea. Smart Passive Income is here to support you as you bring your idea to life.

Let's keep in touch—join the Smart Passive Income email list for free business advice and encouragement as you build your business.

Go to **SMARTPASSIVEINCOME.COM/LIFTOFF** to sign up. You'll get periodic advice on strategies for building your business, recommendations (and the occasional discount) on useful tools I've tested, and case studies from entrepreneurs just like you who have built an online business based on an idea they tested.

I can't wait to see what you can do!

SMARTPASSIVEINCOME.COM/LIFTOFF

publications

SPI PUBLICATIONS, SAN DIEGO

ABOUT THE AUTHOR

Pat Flynn is a popular podcaster, author, and founder of several successful websites, including Smart Passive Income, where he helps people build thriving online businesses. He has been featured in *Forbes* and in *The New York Times* for his work. He calls himself "The Crash Test Dummy of Online Business" because he loves to put himself on the line and experiment with various business strategies so that he can report his findings publicly to his audience. He is also the author of *Let Go*, a memoir about his transition from architecture into entrepreneurship. He speaks on the topics of product validation, audience engagement, and personal branding.

Pat is also an advisor to Pencils of Promise, a nonprofit organization dedicated to building schools in the developing world. Pat lives in San Diego with his wife April and their two children.

TO LEARN MORE ABOUT PAT, GO TO:

SMARTPASSIVEINCOME.COM/ABOUT

HOW to TEST YOUR
NEXT BUSINESS IDEA
so YOU DON'T WASTE
YOUR TIME and MONEY

PAT FLYNN